HAUNTED
LUTON &
DUNSTABLE

HAUNTED
LUTON &
DUNSTABLE

Paul Adams

The History Press

For Tony Broughall –
the original 'Ghost Man' of Luton

About the Author

Paul Adams was born in Epsom, Surrey in 1966 and has been interested in the paranormal since the mid-1970s. Employed as a draughtsman in the UK construction industry for nearly thirty years, he has worked in three haunted buildings but has yet to see a true ghost. As well as the history of psychical research, his main interests at present are in materialisation mediumship and the physical phenomena of Spiritualism. He has contributed articles to several specialist paranormal periodicals and acted as editor and publisher for *Two Haunted Counties* (2010), the memoirs of Luton ghost hunter, Tony Broughall. Adams is the co-author, with Peter Underwood and Eddie Brazil, of *The Borley Rectory Companion* (2009) and *Shadows in the Nave* (2011), and has written *Ghosts & Gallows* (2012), a study of British true crime cases with paranormal connections. He is also an amateur mycologist and viola-player and has lived in Limbury, Luton since 2006.

*Frontispiece: Luton Town Hall from
St George's Square (Eddie Brazil)*

First published 2012
Reprinted 2013

The History Press
The Mill, Brimscombe Port
Stroud, Gloucestershire, GL5 2QG
www.thehistorypress.co.uk

British Library Cataloguing in Publication Data.
A catalogue record for this book is available from the British Library.

ISBN 978 0 7524 6548 7

Typesetting and origination by The History Press
Printed and bound in Great Britain by
Marston Book Services Limited, Didcot

Contents

Acknowledgements

A number of people deserve recognition for their help and assistance with this book. I would like to thank Damien O'Dell, founder of the Anglia Paranormal Investigation Society, not only for his interest in the project and for writing the Foreword, but also for supplying material on a number of his investigations; Kevin Gates for sharing information on his researches into the Clophill case and for allowing me to use material from his original article 'The Caddington Horror'; Dr Elisabeth Adey who provided details of the history of Wardown Park Museum and Chris Grabham for sending through information on Galley Hill; Tony Broughall for discussing his unique experiences of Luton and Bedfordshire ghosts and for allowing me to quote from his published memoirs; Eddie Brazil for his constant support and for taking the superb contemporary photographs; Julian Vince for producing original illustrations; Andi Brooks for supplying information on Bela Lugosi at the Alma Theatre; Howard Chandler for information on local Luton street names; Andrew Fazekas of the Luton Paranormal Society for revisiting his experiences in Ashcroft Park; Rita Goold for her reminiscences of Gina Brealey and Helen Duncan; Bev Creagh at the *Luton News* for help with collecting new local paranormal encounters; the staff at both Luton Central Library and Leagrave Library for providing access to newspaper archives and for obtaining reference books; and Cate Ludlow and Nicola Guy at The History Press. My thanks also go to Jan Fleckney, and to Marion Betts, Janice Newitt, Chris Harkin, Charlie Harkin, Carol Cyl and several other Lutonians who contacted me with details of their own personal experiences of the ghosts of Luton. And, finally, to Aban, Idris, Isa and Sakina, who continue to make everything worthwhile.

Foreword

PARANORMAL researchers have long known that Luton is one of the most haunted towns in England – this book will help to convince those who may be in any doubt about the matter. My own research group, the Anglia Paranormal Investigation Society (APIS), has a number of members who live in Luton. Together we have experienced many examples of anomalous phenomena in this part of Bedfordshire, whilst engaged in our investigations. These incidents remain unexplained. Paul Adams has faithfully documented these extraordinary events, together with scores of others, in *Haunted Luton*.

Luton holds a special place in my affections for a number of reasons. Not least of these was the enthusiastic turnout at Luton Central Library for my talk 'Adventures of a Ghost Hunter' back in 2004, which was attended by 150 local people. This reinforced the fact that Lutonians are interested in their town and its haunted places. *Haunted Luton* is long overdue in my opinion, because Luton has been overlooked in the pantheon of haunted locations, whilst cities and towns such as Edinburgh, London, York, Cambridge and Whitby have claimed the limelight. All have successful, well-attended ghost walks – I see no reason why Luton should not also have its own ghost walk, and a suggestion for just such an event is included in the present book.

During 2009/10, I had an office at Basepoint, in Luton's Stopsley district, where I got to know the area (and its ghosts) quite well. It was a pleasant surprise to read Paul Adams' manuscript and to discover countless true tales of paranormal phenomena, associated with the town, that were completely new to me. The authentic stories have been meticulously researched and are wide-ranging in scope. Their author is a well-respected writer of paranormal books, who lives in Luton and knows his home town intimately. If you live in the Luton area and are interested in its haunted history, this book was written for you. I hope that you enjoy reading it as much as I did.

Damien O'Dell
January 2012

Introduction

PARANORMAL guides such as this one operate on several levels. As a collection of ghostly stories they can be enjoyed with the lights low on a winter's evening, or as a companion to a tour or ghost walk, by day, or more bravely at night. For the historian they contain interesting local records pertaining to people, places and events that would otherwise be forgotten or go unrecorded. For the serious ghost hunter, these volumes comprise a reference library of supernatural experiences that can be used as the basis for detailed study or as plans for future vigils and investigations. Most importantly, these books pose questions that have been asked countless times by intelligent and enquiring minds down innumerable years: do ghosts exist? If they do, what are they, where do they come from and what causes them to appear?

The answer to the first of these questions is undoubtedly 'yes'. There can be no doubt in the mind of anyone who has taken the time to carefully study the vast amount of recorded testimony obtained by serious researchers over many years and involving witnesses of intelligence and integrity, that people *do* see ghosts. What is also

clear is that when people see ghosts, this phenomena falls into different categories – different 'types' of ghost – which often share common aspects but at the same time are also unique events or happenings.

The most ordinary of people see ghosts, often at a time when they least expect it. I have spoken with many people who claim to have had experiences that defy currently accepted scientific thinking and break both social taboos and religious orthodoxy. From a young age I was told about the cyclical haunting that affected the eighteenth-century house of a family friend of my father's where bedclothes were pulled, doors rattled and opened, and a parrot in a cage was moved from one side of a room to the other one night when everyone was asleep. As a schoolboy I spoke with Col. Francis Claridge, the tenant of Sandford Orcas Manor House who showed me a photograph of a ghostly white figure, an 'extra', that had appeared in the background of a snapshot photograph of his daughter taken on the lawn of the house. An office cleaner once described to me how a hazy grey apparition had placed a hand on his shoulder, and a work colleague vividly recalled seeing the figure of a small girl walk out of a wardrobe in a house where he was staying on holiday. The owner of a bungalow built in the garden of what was once described as the 'most haunted house in England' has related to me her experience of seeing a black nun-like apparition walk past an open doorway while she was sitting one evening watching television, waiting for her husband to come home with a Chinese takeaway. My best friend recalls with unshakeable honesty his experiences as a young boy in a house in Stockwell, South London, where footsteps were often heard walking down the stairs and doors opened seemingly by themselves. For this book I have interviewed and spoken with over a dozen people, all who claim to have had contact with the world of the unseen, and you are shortly about to encounter a number of their experiences for yourself. It is no wonder then that the well-known writer and philosopher Colin Wilson has stated that there is as much evidence for the paranormal as there is for atoms and electrons.

Should we be scared of ghosts? It is natural to be frightened of the unknown, but rather I feel we should be fascinated rather than terrified. The paranormal, by its unique nature, has always lent itself to exploitation: the modern chillers of Stephen King and Susan Hill; the classic ghost stories of M.R. James, Algernon Blackwood and Robert Aickman and many others, trace a lineage of fascination with the supernatural back to Poe and Shakespeare. If you can separate the macabre from the reality, then the world of the ghost hunter and the psychical researcher is as fascinating and rewarding as that of the surgeon or the astrophysicist, but who, in their roles as scientists will tell you that, after all, there are no such things as ghosts …

In *Haunted Luton* I have tried to present the paranormal at what could be described as grass-roots level, and show that many people have strange experiences in the most ordinary of daily situations. In some instances I have replaced the names of witnesses with pseudonyms but the identities of all contributors are known to me. As well as Luton itself, I have included a number of cases from the surrounding area including Dunstable and Houghton Regis, as some of the material originating there is particularly interesting and too convincing to pass by without mention. Although this is a book of provincial hauntings and other unexplained Fortean phenomena, I have made comparisons in certain instances with other national, and in a couple of places, international cases, which I feel are particularly pertinent to the discussions in hand. To my mind, the ghosts of Luton are clearly pieces of a wider puzzle which an examination of the bigger picture may one day help to solve.

Which brings us to the answers to the other questions posed above: what ghosts are and where their origins lie. These, as are noted with some frequency throughout this survey, are mysteries that are yet to receive as similar and conclusive an answer as that given to the fundamental question 'do ghosts exist?' We may never know. Perhaps then the last word should be given, somewhat perversely perhaps given his noted scepticism, to the late British science fiction writer and futurist thinker, Arthur C. Clarke, who often paraphrased the biologist J.B.S. Haldane when asked to give an opinion on reincarnation and the paranormal: 'The universe is not only stranger than we imagine, it's stranger than we can imagine.'

Paul Adams
January 2012

one

Ghost Roads

YOU are as likely to have a super-natural encounter on the highways of England as you are in much as the country's numerous haunted houses (which in fact must number tens of thousands), stately homes and castles, and our survey of Luton's ghostly heritage begins with an examination of the most notable stories and reports of paranormal experiences connected with the roads and byways that pass through and around the town and its surrounding area. They include an interesting variety of strange phenomena, apparitional figures and eerie encounters, and one of these particular 'road ghosts' can be considered to be one of the most convincing examples of its kind.

Before the construction of the M1 motorway, which cut through the western outskirts of Luton in the early 1960s, the A5 trunk road, which runs to the south-west of the town up to and through Dunstable and on to Milton Keynes, was together with the A6 further east, the principal route out of London heading north to the Midlands and beyond. The significance of the painting on a former sign hanging outside the Packhorse, a 300-year-old hostelry

and former mortuary house located on the A5 north of Markyate village, depicting as it did a man in cricketing whites complete with cap and cricket bat, may have been lost on many of the drivers and travellers who passed this particular spot. However, the image of this solitary cricketer had connections, both with tragedy and the supernatural, which go back to an event that took place here over forty years ago.

In 1958, a minibus travelling south-bound on the A5 attempted to overtake a car on the stretch of highway close to the Packhorse Inn and came off the road, crashing violently. The bus had been hired by a works' cricket team from Surrey who were returning from a match at Milton Bryan near Woburn. There were several injuries and two fatalities: both Jeremy Rycham and Sidney Moulder of the Kenwood Manufacturing Ltd team were killed at the scene. This event has given rise to belief locally that this part of the A5 between the turn-offs for Flamstead and Markyate is a haunted road, as it appears that on a number of occasions the figure of a solitary cricketer has been seen standing beside or walking in the roadway.

The 300-year-old Packhorse on the A5 trunk road south of Dunstable, where the apparition of a man in cricketing 'whites' has been seen walking in the roadway. (Eddie Brazil)

Dates of sightings and details of witnesses are, as will be seen from a number of other hauntings included in this book, sadly lacking, and appearances of the figure seem to have peaked in the early 1970s as there seem to be no encounters on record after this time. One prominent sighting, by a taxi driver on a Sunday morning, has been dated as occurring either in 1970 or 1973 in published accounts, and in both the driver himself is unnamed. However, both agree that a 6ft-tall figure of a man dressed in white was seen to suddenly step out into the road, causing the driver to brake violently and, unable to avoid a collision, strike the figure which subsequently disappeared. Other undated encounters would seem to be less dramatic in nature, with the brief appearance of the roadside apparition being put down to a local player returning home alone from a nearby match.

As well as the phantom cricketer, this part of the A5 has connections with other hauntings. A mile south of the Packhorse, the trunk road begins a bypass of the village of Markyate at the junction with the B4540 Luton Road, which passes through Slip End before arriving at the south side of Luton at Stockwood Park. Just after the Markyate junction, the stretch of highway where the Luton Road bends sharply and begins a hard climb up towards the outlying houses near Caddington Hall, is known for a single (albeit undated) sighting of the apparition of an old woman wearing a black coat. The claimant to the experience was Mrs Wilkins, a Dunstable housewife, who was driving from Markyate to Slip End around 9 a.m. on a sunny spring morning. As she reached the bend at the bottom of the hill, Mrs Wilkins was alarmed to see what she took to be the solid figure of an elderly woman dressed in black who suddenly stepped out, seemingly from nowhere, into the roadway in front of her car. The figure glanced in her direction but continued on to the other side of the carriageway where to Mrs Wilkins' horror it seemed completely oblivious to a large car transporter which at that moment was coming round the bend towards the Markyate junction. The woman in black was lost to sight and, fearing a horrific accident, Mrs Wilkins pulled over and ran back down the road. However, there was no sign of a fallen pedestrian and the car transporter had carried on its way, the driver having not reacted in any way to the presence of the old lady, which the shocked motorist now realised had in fact been an apparition. The appearance of the Luton Road phantom follows a similar pattern to that of many road ghosts reported around the British Isles which are often consistent in their manifestation: the sudden appearance of the figure stepping out from the kerb-side, the glance made towards the observer as it passes in front of the witness's vehicle, together with the equally rapid disappearance. These apparitions are often described as sinking down (sometimes with an unnerving smile on their faces) and being lost to sight in front of the vehicle or vanishing into the path of oncoming traffic.

The junction of the A5 and the B4540 Luton Road forms the south-west boundary of the grounds of Markyate Cell, a former Tudor manor house originally constructed around 1539 on the site of an earlier priory which had become vacant following the Dissolution of the Monasteries. Markyate Cell is most commonly associated with the Ferrers family and stories attached to the seventeenth-century female highwayman Katherine Ferrers, daughter of the then owner Knighton Ferrers, who was shot and fatally wounded at the age of twenty-five while robbing a coach on Nomansland Common in 1659. Her short but dramatic life story was the basis for the 1945 cinema film *The Wicked Lady*, with Margaret Lockwood in the title role supported by a youthful James Mason as a fellow footpad, and there are several accounts of her ghost being seen in the vicinity of her former home, which was extensively damaged and subsequently rebuilt following a fire that broke out in 1840. Reports of appearances of Katherine Ferrer's apparition are now not surprisingly anecdotal: around 1900, a gamekeeper allegedly fired a shotgun at her mounted figure as it rode along what is now the A5 towards Dunstable, while a year or so later (possibly in 1901), it disrupted an afternoon tea party in the grounds of the house itself. One of the later appearances was again in the garden in the early 1960s, when she was

Katherine Ferrers, whose ghost is said to haunt the grounds and roads around her former home of Markyate Cell.

seen by the daughter of the then owner. Ghostly nuns, connected with the former religious use of the site, are also associated with the grounds of Markyate Cell, but for the serious ghost hunter keen to obtain specific information, firm details are unfortunately scarce.

The anecdotal nature of many reported ghost sightings is one of the problems that confronts anyone attempting to carry out research or further investigation into a specific case or ghostly experience. Another haunting connected with the A5 trunk road in the Luton and Dunstable area is a case in point. On the northern outskirts of Dunstable at Chalk Hill (also known as Puddle Hill), the road passes through a chalk cutting before reaching open farmland on the way to nearby Hockliffe. Here a public footpath that skirts the edge of a now disused quarry between Puddle Hill and Houghton Regis is the setting for what at first appears to be a small slice of local ghost folklore, having the reputation of being haunted by the apparition of a headless Saxon chieftain dressed in full battle armour. The story appeared to be common knowledge, particularly during the inter-war years, but unsurprisingly was not supported by anything other than local rumour, no doubt inspired by the lonely and atmospheric nature of this rural location. However, during the 1950s, a group of local-history enthusiasts who had recently formed themselves into the fledgling Manshead Archaeological Society, made an interesting discovery at a site close to the Puddle Hill cutting that seemed to have some bearing on the stories of the ghostly Saxon lord. A gravesite was unearthed containing the mutilated skeleton of a murdered Saxon man. The remains bore evidence of an ancient wayside murder: the skull was battered and smashed and the

body had been hastily concealed in a tiny shallow grave, the legs broken between the knees and thighs after death as the body had been forced into the ground where it had lain hidden and unknown for several centuries. Perhaps something of this ancient tragedy was able to linger through time and give rise to the stories of the wandering and nameless ghost. At least there is a link, albeit a tenuous one, with an actual verifiable event that may or may not have a connection with this particular local haunting.

Other roads around Luton have the reputation for similar ghost stories. To the south-east, the approach from Wheathampstead along the B653 Lower Harpenden Road at New Mill End is said to be the haunt of an eerie black figure carrying a lantern, as well as the apparition of a man in a tricorn hat riding an equally spectral galloping horse. What little evidence there is for both these occurrences would appear to date from many years back, with the result that credible sightings are non-existent. However, the sighting of what could be described as a corpse light (often termed a 'spook light' in America) was reported as being seen by a correspondent of the *Herts Advertiser* newspaper around the beginning of the 1900s, where it was connected with the proximity of the known grave or death site of a local suicide victim.

In contrast to these tales, for the next two cases in our 'road ghost' survey, we are fortunate in having dated and detailed accounts of unexplained phenomena by two credible and unbiased witnesses that together provide convincing, and it must be said unnerving, evidence of the reality of the paranormal in action.

The first of these incidents dates from the early 1960s and involves Tony Broughall, arguably Luton's first

Luton ghost busters, Tony and Georgina Broughall, photographed at Hitchin Priory in 1979. (Home Counties Newspapers Ltd, Luton)

serious ghost hunter and the first person to compile detailed county-wide surveys of haunted locations in both Bedfordshire and Hertfordshire. Broughall was born in Ashburnham Road in Luton in 1932, and during his working life has had an eclectic mix of careers which includes spells as a jazz drummer, a cinema projectionist, civil servant and funeral director. Christened 'The Ghost Man' by the *Luton News*, as a paranormalist, he was a member of both the Society for Psychical Research and the Ghost Club, and during the 1970s,

accompanied by his wife Georgina, a natural clairvoyant, Tony Broughall undertook a number of original and detailed investigations of local spontaneous cases, accounts of which were published as part of his paranormal gazetteer *Two Haunted Counties* (2010). It is in these memoirs that he describes what was his first – and most unsettling – experience with supernormal phenomena.

Before the urban sprawl of the northern outskirts of Luton and Dunstable reached Houghton Regis during the 1970s, the boundaries of this former Domesday village were less blurred than they are today, and the area retained much of its rural atmosphere. In 1963, Sundon Road was a remote and unlit byway surrounded by fields where Tony Broughall often found himself walking alone in the early hours of the morning. At the time Broughall was working as a projectionist in Dunstable, and had recently met his future wife, Georgina Richer, who lived with her parents on a new estate in Houghton Regis. In order to spend as much time together, Tony would often forego catching the night bus back to Luton and would walk home through the dark and lonely countryside. It was during one of these excursions that he had an unnerving encounter with the supernatural. In his memoirs, Broughall describes the incident in the following way:

One clear spring night I had just left [Georgina's] parents' home in Recreation Road and was about 50 yards along Sundon Road when a black shape appeared to cross the roadway from right to left. I estimated it was approximately 50 yards ahead of me. All I could see was what appeared to be the head and shoulders of a figure as it was silhouetted against the skyline. I thought it odd that there was no sound to be heard but concluded that it was someone riding a bicycle towards the village and I had seen him or her as the rider took the bend a little further down the road. A few seconds later I reached the same bend, fully expecting to see a rear light disappearing into the distance, or at least a fellow traveller clearly in view against the background of lights at the road junction, but there was nothing to be seen. The road was empty but I was certain someone or something had crossed

the road only a little way in front of me … A week or so later, again on a clear and fine night, I was approaching the junction at the Chequers [pub] when I was suddenly and violently pushed towards a muddy ditch adjacent to the footpath on which I was walking. I saw and heard nothing but the impact was quite deliberate and obviously calculated to pitch me in the slimy water, possibly with injuries as well. Again there was nothing to account for my experience, and certainly no trace of anyone anywhere to be seen.

Shaken by his experience, Broughall continued to make his night-time trips until, a short time later, another incident proved too much and made him decide to take the last bus home:

Again it was in the early hours of the morning when I left Recreation Road and there was a fine drizzle falling as I hurried along. I had just passed Leafields when I became aware of an eerie tuneless whistling steadily overtaking me as I strode along. The notes were aimless and jumbled and whoever or whatever was producing them seemed in no need to pause to draw breath. As the sound came closer I glanced round, but in the drizzle and darkness I could see nothing so I quickened my pace as I headed towards the distant lights at the Chequers road junction. The whistling continued to close the gap between us at the same steady rate despite my increase in pace. A few seconds later I could sense it was only a few feet behind me and at that moment my nerve went and I ran the hundred yards into the relative safety of the yellow street lights at the junction. Looking back, there was only the patter of the rain and nothing to be seen.

Tony Broughall was not the only person to experience unusual happenings in lonely Sundon Road at the time. A short while afterwards, the future ghost hunter met a young motorcyclist who claimed to have seen a similar unidentifiable black shape on the same stretch of road which appeared to step out of nowhere, forcing the rider to brake violently and lose control of his machine. Broughall was unable to explain his experience. It was, like the best and convincing incidents of paranormal activity, spontaneous and uninvited. At the time Tony Broughall had no interest in ghosts and hauntings, was not concerned with or thinking about psychic matters, and it was to be nearly ten years before he became involved in organised psychical research and began carrying out his own investigations. As such, the haunting of Sundon Road remains inexplicable and short-lived; no other reports of similar activity from the time have survived and today the area has become vastly altered with new housing developments.

It should be mentioned in passing that close to Sundon Road is Drury Lane, another of Houghton Regis' haunted byways, known for the apparition of a young girl that has allegedly been seen a number of times since the 1930s. Said to be the ghost of a child knocked down and killed while returning home from a Sunday-school class, evidence seems today to be almost wholly anecdotal, apart from one sighting that took place during the 1970s. Charles Doerrer, a sergeant in the United States Air Force then stationed at Chicksands Priory near Shefford (itself a well-known haunted site), together with his wife Lorraine, had what is to date the most modern encounter with this particular ghost while walking through Houghton Regis village after an evening out. The hour was late when, as they strolled together around the edge of the village green, the couple noticed a small child wearing a simple white dress but no shoes approaching them along the main road. The child passed by them, seemingly oblivious to the Doerrers' presence and, turning into Drury Lane, was lost to sight. Concerned for her safety they followed but the young girl, whose age they estimated as being between five and seven years, was nowhere to be seen. Charles Doerrer, later a member of the Ghost Club during the presidency of writer and ghost hunter Peter Underwood, was a reliable witness whose testimony should not be dismissed lightly. He was convinced that he and Lorraine Doerrer saw the ghost child and subsequently corresponded with Tony Broughall about his experience.

What is in fact arguably not only a candidate for one of the Luton area's most impressive ghost stories, but also one of the most convincing spontaneous cases of modern times, took place three miles to the east of Houghton Regis only a few years after the experience of Charles Doerrer and his wife. The phenomenon of the phantom hitch-hiker, the mysterious spectral traveller who disappears into thin air after being picked up by a passing motorist or motorcyclist, is a category of paranormal encounter that is known the world over – countries as diverse and wide apart as Sweden, Pakistan, Canada, Korea and South Africa all have their own individual and specific hitch-hiker tales. The experience of Bedfordshire motorist Roy Fulton, however, ranks as one of the most compelling and thought-provoking examples of this particular roadside phantom, and the case is chilling and fascinating in equal measure.

Late on the evening of 12 October 1979, Fulton, a twenty-six year-old carpet-fitter from Dunstable, was driving home after playing in a darts match at a pub in

Leighton Buzzard. It was a cold misty Friday night and, like Tony Broughall over fifteen years before, notions of ghosts and the supernatural were far from Roy Fulton's mind: being an avid Liverpool FC fan, he was casting his thoughts ahead to the following day's match and the prospects of his favourite team. Driving along an unlit section of Station Road on the outskirts of Stanbridge, Fulton saw in the glare of the Mini van's headlights the figure of a young man standing on the nearside pavement thumbing for a lift and, guessing he was either going to Totternhoe or Dunstable, decided to pull over. Slowing down he stopped in front of the hitch-hiker who responded by walking along the pavement towards the van. He was casually dressed in dark trousers and wore a dark-coloured jumper with an open white-collared shirt. Nothing seemed out of the ordinary; the man looked pale but the only thing that struck Fulton as slightly unusual was the shape of the youth's face, which he later described as being 'unusually long'. The hiker opened the van door and got in, but when asked where he wanted to go, his only response was to point ahead further down the misty road. Fulton let in the Mini's clutch and the van pulled away.

The journey continued in silence for some minutes until Fulton decided to offer the youth a cigarette. It was the point where what had been a completely ordinary and familiar situation suddenly crossed over a threshold into the strange and frightening world of the unknown. As Fulton later recalled, 'I leant forward and picked up the packet of cigarettes [and] turned round to

Drury Lane, Houghton Regis, where USAF Sergeant Charles Doerrer and his wife saw the apparition of a young girl in a white dress. (Paul Adams)

Station Road, Stanbridge: the author stands on the spot where one night in 1979, Dunstable carpet-fitter Roy Fulton picked up a phantom hitch-hiker. (Isa Adams)

offer the lad one, *and that man or boy was not sitting there.*' Stunned, Fulton pulled the Mini to a halt and, turning on the interior light looked into the back, thinking that the youth had somehow climbed into the rear of the van. There was nothing there – Roy Fulton was completely alone.

Now terrified, Fulton drove 'like a bat out of Hell' to his local pub, the Glider in Lowther Road, Dunstable, where his entry into the bar, shaking and ashen-faced, was greeted initially with some levity by the landlord, Bill Stone, who asked jokily, 'What's the matter, Roy? Have you seen a ghost, or what?'

'I have,' Fulton replied, 'I have seen a ghost,' and, after a large whisky, proceeded to tell the strange and disturbing story.

Two things haunted Fulton about his experience: the possibility that the eerie pale-faced youth was somehow part of an earlier traffic accident which had not been reported to the police, and secondly, in the tradition of fictional ghost stories, that the sad silent figure would somehow follow him home. In order to address these issues, later the same night Roy Fulton went to Dunstable police station where Inspector Rowland was told the same account. Accustomed to hearing all manner of unusual stories, Rowland was unable to offer any explanation – no accident involving a hitch-hiker had been reported on that section of Station Road, either that day or in the proceeding weeks; neither, to the policeman's knowledge, had a similar account to Fulton's about a disappearing figure been local knowledge in the area. Fulton went home with his wife Sheila, the experience still weighing on his mind, to the point that the couple slept with the bedroom light on in order to alleviate the carpet-fitter's fear that the ghost would return.

Fulton's story made both local and national headlines – the *Dunstable Gazette* and later the *Sunday Express* picked up the story. All those who came into contact with Roy Fulton and heard him describe his experience were impressed with his sincerity, making the idea that he was perpetrating an elaborate hoax an unlikely one. Fulton was later interviewed by writer and researcher Michael Goss (who subsequently published what is to date the most complete and detailed account of the incident) and in 1985 took part in the respected television documentary series *Arthur C. Clarke's World of Strange Powers*, in which he was interviewed on camera and featured in a reconstruction of his experience. On both occasions he told the same story without any deviations or embellishments – that one night in October 1979, he took a ghost

Roy Fulton, photographed during the early 1980s. His encounter with a phantom hitch-hiker remains one of the most convincing examples on record. (Michael Goss)

for a ride. 'There's obviously someone [*sic*] got in that motor,' Fulton would later state, 'and I do not know to this day what it was.'

Can we explain Roy Fulton's compelling and eerie experience? Was the person who climbed inside his Mini van the spirit of a dead pedestrian, some paranormally induced hallucination, or a figment of his imagination? In the 1940s, British mathematician and psychical researcher George N.M. Tyrrell developed a theory of apparitions based on data collected as part of the Census of Hallucinations, the first large-scale questionnaire into sightings of ghosts and associated paranormal experiences carried out by the then fledgling Society for Psychical Research (SPR) in the closing decade of the nineteenth century. As part of his thesis – delivered as the seventh Myers Memorial Lecture before the Society in 1942 – Tyrrell devised a concept that he termed the 'Perfect Apparition', an imaginary collation of the many reported aspects (nineteen in total) of ghostly figures and forms that had been reported (and are still being reported to this day) as being experienced by members of the public over many years. These characteristics included the complete three-dimensional reality of the apparition, its ability to pick up real objects and open and close doors, touch people, be visible in mirrors, appear unexpectedly and ultimately suddenly vanish without trace, as well as having some aspect to it that on reflection strikes the person seeing the ghost as slightly odd or not quite right. Although Tyrrell's creation was simply a way of demonstrating the bizarre and seemingly unknowable rules behind the numerous well reported and documented sightings of apparitions, many aspects of his theoretical 'perfect ghost' seem to apply to the strange silent man that got into Roy Fulton's van that October night in the late

1970s: the living 'flesh and blood' quality of the figure, the way it opened and closed the van door, its visibility in the vehicle's headlights, as well as the figure's curiously long and pale-looking face. Did the young carpet-fitter encounter the 'Perfect Apparition' on the misty byways near Dunstable all those years ago? What actually happened that night we will now never know for sure – Roy Fulton died in December 2002 at the age of forty-nine, taking the secrets of the phantom hitch-hiker with him.

Lonely country lanes and byways seem the ideal haunt for ghosts and mysterious phantoms that surprise and waylay the unsuspecting traveller. However, across Britain the roads and thoroughfares of towns and cities are equally prone to ghostly activity and those of Luton are no exception. At least two phantom figures are known to have made their presence felt here, although it must be said that neither have been reported now for many years, and the reasons for their inactivity, as with those governing their appearance, are mysterious and, like the powers that control the appearance of all ghosts, are at present unknown. Ghost hunting is very much a discipline of phenomenology – researchers and investigators simply aim to collect information regarding paranormal experiences as accurately and truthfully as possible; theories as to what actually cause these experiences are many, but the real truth, as was observed by Arthur C. Clarke in the Introduction, may always be beyond us.

A gas supply was first laid on in Luton during the early 1830s by the newly established Luton Gas & Coke Co. whose stirring motto *Ex Fumo Dare Lucem* – Out of Smoke Came Light – became a familiar local slogan. For much of the twentieth century, the company's gas works occupied a large wedge-shaped tract of land north-west of the town centre between the Bedford to London railway and the branch line to Dunstable. Today the gasometers have gone, the area has been redeveloped and the popular Sainsbury's and Lidl supermarkets now occupy the site. Back in the early 1960s, the Francis Street gas works were still in use, an unlikely spot for an encounter with the supernatural it would seem, but ghosts operate by their own rules and it was here, in the summer of 1961, that two of the works' employees had a strange and possibly unprecedented experience. Sixty-five-year-old Bert Fleckney, together with another night worker, Jack Boutwood, who was in his mid-thirties, claimed to have seen the apparition of a tall woman of almost Amazonian proportions dressed in shining white robes walking or gliding along the thoroughfare of Crawley Road near its junction with Francis Street. Fleckney, who noticed the figure first while standing on the street corner during a cigarette break, called to his colleague who also saw the ghostly form, close enough to later describe it as being around forty years of age, with long, jet-black hair and having a strange 'translucent' appearance. Both men followed the apparition which drifted along Bury Park Road before passing underneath the Waldeck Road railway bridge where it seemingly turned into Highbury Road before disappearing. The ghostly woman was not actually seen to vanish or fade away but simply could not be found by either of the two gas workers, or by the crew of a patrolling police car who on being flagged down by Fleckney and Boutwood made an unsuccessful search of the area.

Ghost hunters describe this kind of experience as a collective apparition whereby a ghostly figure (or the hallucination of one) is seen by more than one person at the same time. Such an

Waldeck Road in Bury Park. In 1961, a bizarre female apparition encountered by two Luton gas works employees was seen drifting under the railway bridge before disappearing into Highbury Road on the left. (Eddie Brazil)

occurrence increases the strength of the evidence for paranormality as subsequent investigators are not reliant on the sole testimony of a single witness – we only have Roy Fulton's word that he picked up the eerie Stanbridge hitch-hiker, although the background and subsequent reporting of his experience lend considerable weight to his encounter being a genuine one. What actually happened that night will remain a mystery, but Fulton clearly believed that for a few brief minutes he picked up and spoke with a ghost. The history of psychical research is littered with many convincing reports of collective sightings of ghostly forms and figures. In 1987, four students visiting the ruins of Thetford Priory near Bury St Edmunds in Norfolk all saw the figure of a monk

dressed in flowing black robes descending a staircase in the vicinity of the former Prior's house. As the men approached, the apparition retreated up the stairway and suddenly, both the black-clad form *and* the staircase itself suddenly vanished: both had been a paranormal vision. A more famous encounter of this kind took place in the grounds of Borley Rectory, the notorious 'most haunted house in England' in Essex, during the opening decade of the twentieth century. On 28 July 1900, four of the Bull sisters saw the apparition of the famous 'Borley nun' which was observed for some minutes in full daylight moving silently across the rectory lawn before eventually disappearing. The origins of the Borley ghost, like the Amazonian ghost reported years later by Bert Fleckney and

Jack Boutwood, are obscure, although in the case of the Luton phantom, local ghost hunters Tony Broughall and William King have both linked this particular incident with two other nearby hauntings: a nun-like figure observed in the Dallow Road area on one occasion during the 1940s, and a similar apparition known as the 'White Woman of Downs Road', which according to Tony Broughall was reported with some regularity in that part of the town between 1900 and the end of the 1920s.

For anyone who has actively studied the history of ghostly activity in Britain, it is clear that just as easily as old hauntings fade away or become inactive, new ghosts are ready to appear and take their place. The A505 Vauxhall Way skirts Luton town centre to the east, channelling busy through traffic from the M1 motorway north-eastwards towards Hitchin and Letchworth. While collecting material for the present book, I was given an account of an encounter with a roadside apparition that took place here during the 1990s. Despite the modernity of the incident, like many ghosts of old, this is third-hand and anecdotal in nature, but, if true, shows that spontaneous encounters with the paranormal are continually taking place amongst the mundane day-to-day normality of ordinary life. A motorist, driving along the Vauxhall Way bypass early one evening, was passing by the car factory site when suddenly, seemingly out of nowhere, the figure of a cyclist appeared directly in front of the car. Like the taxi driver mentioned earlier in connection with Markyate's phantom cricketer, the male driver was unable to react in time and struck the figure, feeling the impact before bringing the vehicle to an emergency stop. Shaken, the unnamed driver got out and looked about for the fallen rider, but both the person and his bicycle had completely vanished.

Spontaneous cases, such as the ones we have briefly encountered, can offer some of the best evidence for the reality of a hidden unseen world of seemingly limitless and unknowable proportions that manifests itself through the appearance of ghosts and apparitions. People see and experience paranormal phenomena when they least expect it: Tony Broughall's invisible assailant, Roy Fulton's sinister and silent passenger, even the bizarre gas works phantom encountered by Bert Fleckney and Jack Boutwood. All these experiences were, for the people involved, unprecedented and unplanned. What happens though when people deliberately set out to make contact with the hidden world beyond the veil? Some of the answers lie in the tales from the séance room, and it is this aspect of Luton's paranormal heritage that we will explore next …

two

Spiritualism
and Mediumship

LUTON has a strong connection with the Spiritualist movement and its phenomena that covers many years. Way back in 1848, on the other side of the Atlantic, strange poltergeist-type disturbances in the small cabin home of the Fox family in Hydesville, New York State, was the catalyst that ushered in the era of Modern Spiritualism, a new age of astonishing abilities and seemingly organised communication with the dead and departed, through the development of psychic human powers and mediumship. The Fox sisters, three young American women, became the first professional mediums and as others soon found they were able to develop the same abilities, Spiritualism swept the country, eventually coming to Britain in the early 1850s where the Victorian craze for séances and table-tipping became a society phenomenon. Spiritualist churches and meeting places were eventually established in most major towns and cities. Many were simple affairs, often single rooms above shop premises, such as the church above the former Home & Colonial Stores in Luton town centre, now long since demolished and buried

underneath the Arndale shopping mall. The Spiritualist church in Grove Road, now part of the SNU (Spiritualists' National Union), is the town's most long-standing centre, while for several years Spiritualist services, including regular Saturday demonstrations of clairvoyance, were held at another house in Bury Park, run by the Brealey family, of whom we will hear more about shortly. Two prominent Luton Spiritualists in the years following the end of the Second World War were Mrs Suzanne Smith, a Frenchwoman with an English husband who lived in the New Bedford Road, and Jesse John Hunt, a local journalist and sports reporter who established a Spiritualist meeting house in Compton Avenue, close to Leagrave railway station.

Séances, often held as part of home circles in private houses in semi-dark and blackout conditions, have been a cornerstone of Spiritualist practices since the movement's beginnings in Hydesville. Spirit communication is effected in varying ways according to the abilities or powers of the particular medium taking part, the most common being 'direct voice' whereby a spirit person speaks to a circle member or a relative present in the room using the medium's own vocal cords. In the first half of the twentieth century, and continuing through the post-war years into the early 1960s, trumpet mediumship was often demonstrated. This involved a cone-shaped, megaphone-like device made of cellophane or cardboard, placed in the centre of the circle and which, when energised by the presence of a spirit visitor, would rise and float unaided in the darkness, passing around the circle. The voice of the ghostly communicator would be heard through the cone, often in whispers, but sometimes loud and clear. The movement and position of the speaking trumpet was made visible by bands of luminous material or paint placed on both ends of the cone.

Then, as now, the rarest type of séance room phenomena was *materialisation*, a form of physical mediumship which involves the temporary creation of solid spirit forms and figures through the production and manipulation of a mysterious substance called 'ectoplasm', said to exude from the bodily orifices of the medium – ears, nose and mouth – as well as from the solar plexus, and which is used to create temporary living facsimiles of departed relatives. Today there are only a handful of these alleged materialisation mediums who give public demonstrations, but in what could be described as the twentieth century's golden age of Spiritualist mediumship – the inter-war years – they were more common, but equally as controversial. The supposed need for darkness in materialisation séances, said to be essential for the successful production of ectoplasm, has been the cover for much séance-room fraud over the years; several mediums were exposed in trickery and there are some paranormal researchers (as well as the ardent disbelievers and sceptics) who feel that it

is unlikely that any medium from the past ever produced a genuine materialisation.

One such physical medium with a Luton connection was John Boaden Webber, a former Welsh miner, known throughout the Spiritualist community as Jack Webber. By the time of his premature death, in London on 9 March 1940 at the age of thirty-three, Webber had built up a formidable reputation as an evidential trumpet and materialisation medium, and had given many public séances. His abilities, despite being championed by healer Harry Edwards, who took infra-red photographs of Webber's ectoplasm at the Balham Psychical Society, were treated with suspicion by such figures as Harry Price and Dr Eric Dingwall, both leading paranormal researchers of the time, and for

A portrait of Spiritualist medium John Boaden 'Jack' Webber'. (Leon Isaacs)

us today, decades later, he remains a strange and enigmatic figure.

Like many other streets in the centre of Luton, Rothesay Road has changed considerably over the years. The north side of the street heading east from the junction with Napier Road has been redeveloped and the Victorian houses that were once there have been replaced with office blocks. However, some of the original terraced houses still survive, and it may have been to one of these that Jack Webber travelled from London in order to hold a private materialisation séance in the days shortly before the outbreak of the Second World War.

In the home of Luton Spiritualist Jack Keitley, Webber was tied into a Windsor chair and the buttons of his jacket were sewn together with thread before the lights were extinguished. In the darkness, spirit voices were heard as Webber's trumpets rose and floated around the room. At one point during the proceedings, the medium's spirit control announced that the sitters would be given physical evidence of Webber's supernatural abilities and a red light was switched on to show the medium tied to his seat and apparently immobile in a deep trance. When the light was removed, the voice of the spirit guide announced that the medium was being dematerialised and turned upside down so that his feet were touching the ceiling. After a few seconds the light was turned back on and the assembled sitters saw Webber as before, still tied into his chair but with his jacket stripped from his back which lay on the floor with the buttonholes still sewn together. However, on the distempered ceiling was a clear impression of a man's shoe which, when inspected at the end of the séance, was found to match the footwear of Jack Webber exactly. For Jack Keitley it was astonishing proof of the power of the spirit world, and the ghostly footprint on the ceiling remained there for the rest of his life – it may

Jack Webber in action in the late 1930s, roped into a chair during a blackout séance. During a meeting at a house in Rothesay Road, Luton, the medium was allegedly turned upside down by spirit forces, and left a footprint on the ceiling. (Harry Edwards)

still be there today if Keitley's house is one of the original houses which still stands.

Another materialisation medium more well known than Jack Webber was Scotland's Helen Duncan who was famously imprisoned four years after the Welshman's death, following an Old Bailey trial that made newspaper headlines across the country. Seemingly caught red-handed in fraud at a séance at a Spiritualist church in Copnor Road, Portsmouth in January 1944, Mrs Duncan was charged with obtaining money by false pretences and, more famously, under the obscure Witchcraft Act of 1735, for pretending to summon the spirits of the dead. What was described as the 'trial of

Rothesay Road, where the 'footprint on the ceiling' séance took place shortly before the outbreak of the Second World War. (Eddie Brazil)

the century' lasted eight days. Found guilty, Helen Duncan was sentenced to nine months in Holloway Prison. Much has been written over the years concerning the mediumship of Mrs Duncan, and it remains a highly controversial subject. Before the Portsmouth fiasco she was found guilty of fraudulent practices in Edinburgh in 1933 and, much later, police were involved in a raid on another of her séances at a house in Nottingham in 1956, an event that some Spiritualists believe brought about her death, at the age of sixty, five weeks later. However, there are many published testimonials to the genu-

ineness of her abilities and, as such, she continues to fascinate. For several years an internet campaign has lobbied the British government to grant a posthumous free pardon for her wartime conviction, while her séance room activities were recently reinvestigated for a modern audience by *Blackadder* actor Tony Robinson, and broadcast on Channel 4 television in December 2009 under the title *The Blitz Witch*. Surprisingly, this famous medium has strong ties with the twentieth-century Spiritualist scene in Luton.

Georgina Duncan was the youngest of Helen Duncan's ten children. She met her future husband George Brealey at a football match when he was in the King's Own Scottish Borderers and stationed in Edinburgh in 1942. Brealey himself had psychic abilities and eventually became a demonstrating clairvoyant. The couple married but George Brealey never himself attended one of his mother-in-law's séances, although according to his wife, when he was first introduced to Mrs Duncan at the family home, the medium went into trance and spoke with the voice of her spirit guide, Albert. He imparted information to the young soldier concerning family matters, unknown to him at the time, that were con-firmed as being entirely accurate by an aunt three years later. After their marriage, and as George's mediumship began to develop, the Brealeys took an active part in Spiritualist meetings and in the mid-1970s moved to Bedfordshire, where for several years they ran the Christian Spiritualist Sanctuary at No.

No. 47a Leagrave Road in Luton's Bury Park. In the mid-1970s, Gena Brealey, daughter of the famous physical medium Helen Duncan, ran a Spiritualist centre here with her husband, George Brealey, a practising clairvoyant. (Eddie Brazil)

The famous materialisation medium, Helen Duncan (1898-1956), who was reunited with her daughter, Gena Brealey, during a séance in Leicester in 1982.

47a Leagrave Road in Luton. The house sur-vives and is today used as an Islamic centre.

In 1983, the Spiritualist weekly *Psychic News* ran a front-page article describ-ing astonishing séance-room phenomena taking place in the home of Leicester-based medium and psychic investigator Rita Goold. Under the headline 'Materialised figures appear at home circle', the news-paper's assistant editor, Alan Cleaver, described the experiences of Alan Crossley, a well-known English Spiritualist, who had attended several blackout séances and was convinced that a number of full-form apparitions had appeared in the room while the medium Rita had been in trance – they included Crossley's own wife; Raymond Lodge, the son of physicist and radio pio-neer Sir Oliver Lodge (himself a noted paranormal investigator) who had been killed during the First World War; and Rita

Goold's grandmother who materialised wearing a beautiful lace dress. Cleaver had attended several séances the previous year and in 1987 summarised his experiences in an article published in the paranormal research group ASSAP's (Association for the Scientific Study of Anomalous Phenomena) journal *Anomaly*. In this he posed the question, 'What constitutes proof of life after death?' and went on to personally state that, 'the most convincing evidence I have witnessed was when Gena [*sic*] Brealey spoke for about an hour to her dead mother Helen Duncan through medium Rita Goold'.

Alan Crossley had known Helen Duncan personally. As a young man he had attended several of her séances, and in 1976 published a biography, *The Story of Helen Duncan*, who he described as 'the greatest physical medium in psychic history'. Crossley was convinced that one of the materialised forms he had spoken with in Leicester and who claimed to be the deceased Scotswoman was exactly who she said she was. According to the report in *Psychic News*, he and the spirit woman had reminisced over several incidents known only to Crossley and the martyred medium, and the materialisation's voice, with its heavy Scots accent, was exactly as he remembered Mrs Duncan speaking.

The opportunity to prove conclusively if Crossley was indeed correct came when, without knowing that her mother was allegedly materialising in the Goold circle, Gina Brealey attended a service at one of the Spiritualist churches in Leicester where she met Barry Jeffrey, one of the circle sitters who himself had attended séances given by Jack Webber in the 1930s. Jeffrey and journalist Alan Cleaver realised that it was possible to carry out a unique experiment by holding a test séance at which Gina would be able to confirm or deny whether in fact the great Helen Duncan had actually returned from beyond the grave. This took place in August 1982, with astonishing results. In his report, Cleaver described the dramatic opening moments of the sitting:

> We lay our hands on the small table and it began to tilt. The light was turned out and the table continued its gyrations. Some apports (paranormally produced objects) were felt to land on the table and eventually we put the light back on. The apports were several deep red carnations and a single red rose which had been placed in front of Gena [*sic*]. Gena broke down in tears and cried, 'What greater proof could I have?' She revealed that at her mother's funeral she had placed a single red rose – unbeknown to other relatives and friends – in her mother's hands in the coffin and whispered, 'I love you.' Years later a medium had told her of this (seemingly relaying the message from Helen) and also said that one day her mother would return the red rose to her. Now the rose had returned …

Later, the heavily accented voice of the deceased medium herself was heard by the sitters speaking through the cardboard trumpet which, like the séances of Jack Webber decades before, had risen from the floor and was seen by the luminous strips attached to the open ends to float around the blacked-out room. Gina Brealey engaged the voice in conversation for more than an hour, and stated afterwards that there was no doubt it was her dead mother communicating. 'It was difficult to follow carefully … because of the use of unfamiliar Scottish slang and because they spoke about people and events of which I, and the rest of the sitters, had no knowledge,' Cleaver reported.

'I was quite convinced she would not be afraid to denounce the voice if it was not her mother. But to make sure, I rang Gena three days after the séance and she reiterated there was no doubt ... There were no 'difficult' moments during the test séance and the conversation flowed freely and easily.' Before her death, Gina Brealey published a book, *The Two Worlds of Helen Duncan* (1985), that included recollections of her childhood with the great medium including the effect the notorious war-time trial had on her mother's reputation, as well as the events which lead up to her last séance in Nottingham in 1956. Gina's involvement in the events at Leicester in 1982 remain a little known but compelling body of evidence for the reality of survival after death and the channelling of deceased persons through the rare abilities of gifted psychic persons.

A Hertfordshire-based medium familiar to Lutonians during the 1970s was Rose Gladden. Primarily regarded as a psychic healer, Mrs Gladden, a former *Psychic News* 'Spiritualist of the Year', was a Londoner born in Edmonton in 1919, who, together with her husband Peter, ran a healing sanctuary in nearby Letchworth and also held open public-healing sessions on occ asion in Luton Town Hall. Paranormal researchers often involve mediums in order to add a Spiritualist dimension to the investigation of haunted places and, as such, Rose accompanied Luton ghost hunter Tony Broughall to a number of sites across the region, including Chicksands Priory near Shefford and the Fox & Duck pub on the village green at Therfield; places where both medium and investigator were rewarded for their efforts with ghostly phenomena. These visits often involved 'rescue circles', whereby troubled or earthbound spirits were encouraged by the psychics taking part to abandon

Medium and healer Rose Gladden (1920–1991), a frequent visitor to Luton during the 1970s, photographed during a ghost hunt at Chicksands Priory. (Home Counties Newspapers Ltd, Luton)

their haunts and, through this release, move on to higher realms.

In June 1975, Rose and Peter Gladden together with Tony and Georgina Broughall, accompanied by Ghost Club and Society for Psychical Research member Alan Roper, held a night-time vigil in a car-repair workshop on the outskirts of Dunstable, where for several months strange and unnerving incidents of a paranormal nature had been disturbing and upsetting the staff. At that time the Downs Garage in Tring Road was owned by Bill and Anne Howe together with their business partner George Hammond, and for five years since taking over the premises in 1970 nothing untoward or remotely supernatural had taken place. However, throughout 1975 the Howes, their secretary Tricia Hambling and several mechanics employed at the garage, all reported unusual happenings. These included overpowering feelings of being watched, unnatural sensations of coldness, and the sound of footsteps coming from parts of the building known to be empty at the time. Bill Howe also received a violent blow to the face while sleeping alone one night on the premises, while their guard dog, which normally behaved in a bold and aggressive manner, was found on one occasion cowering behind blankets which it had seemingly dragged in front of its kennel to block the opening. After this it refused to go into the workshop at night, unless accompanied by one of the staff. A first floor storeroom seemed to be the focus of the disturbances, and at the time the Howes were made aware of a local story concerning a former owner that may have had some connection with the then present haunting.

In the company of the ghost hunters, Rose Gladden toured the haunted premises and gave her impressions of various parts of the building. She came to the conclusion that several earthbound spirits were present and that these were the source of the disturbances. In the downstairs workshop the medium described the presence of a young man with a burnt face who had been killed in a motorcycle accident, and who had returned to the garage to find his machine which had at one time been taken there for repairs. It was his footsteps that were heard in this part of the building. Most of the paranormal activity was located upstairs and here Mrs Gladden described several entities that were aware of their presence. These included a middle-aged man who on a psychic level made himself felt by appearing as a bluish haze, and three people who had died in a car crash and whose vehicle had been stored in the garage while the accident was being investigated. Like the young motorcyclist, they were unaware that they had died and were holding on to the earth plane in limbo. Georgina Broughall together with Rose and Peter Gladden held an impromptu 'rescue' session in the hope that some of the entities would be able to move on from their present state; Mrs Gladden felt that the young motor-cycle rider was the most responsive to this and that he was leaving her and would soon be gone from the building.

Reports of other unusual happenings continued to come out of the Downs Garage during the 1970s. These included the paranormal movement of tyres in the workshop and the turning of the pages of a ledger lying on a desk, in full view of two witnesses, who were seated on the other side of the room. The building subsequently underwent renovation and alterations, although the owners continued to hear noises and experience sensations of a presence in the area of the former first-floor storeroom that appeared unaf-fected by the physical alterations. Often this kind of building work affects the strange and at present unknowable proc-esses behind hauntings that take place in houses and buildings. During the 1980s, I worked in a former dairy in Richmond Road, Kingston-upon-Thames, which had been converted into offices and where sev-eral years previously a regular cleaner had reported experiencing unusual happen-ings, including the appearance of a grey man or figure which had stood behind him and on one occasion made an attempt to place a hand on his shoulder. Following building work on the ground floor, which involved replacing a small kitchen area with a ladies' toilet, the figure was not seen again, although the building continued to retain a distinctive atmosphere and at least one member of staff was unwilling to spend any time alone in a small room up on the second floor where the haunting presence may possibly have relocated itself.

Luton's association with Spiritualism and the world of the séance room has continued steadily into the new millennium. In 1999, the Society for Psychical Research published what amounted to one of the most astonishing – if not *the* most astonishing – document in its then 118-year history. 'The Scole Report'. Written by three of the country's most respected and experienced paranormal researchers, it chronicled the investigation of an organised series of séance-room meetings that took place in a small Norfolk village near the town of Diss throughout the early 1990s. Known as the 'Scole Experiment', this proved to be the last great demonstration of physical mediumship in the twentieth century, and the records of the three investigators – Prof. Arthur Ellison, Prof. David Fontana and Montague Keen – contain accounts of eerie, mind-blowing phenomena seemingly providing conclusive proof of survival after death and discarnate communication from beyond the grave. It includes the materialisation of solid forms and figures, incredible spirit lights, independent voices, the movement of objects, as well as demonstrations of matter-through-matter deemed impossible by traditional scientific orthodoxy.

Montague Keen, a former journalist and farmer and an SPR member for over forty years, was convinced of the reality of the implications of the Scole Experiment and considered the phenomena he personally experienced in Norfolk as genuinely paranormal. Keen was one of Scole's most forthright supporters, particularly when his and his co-authors' report was challenged by critics and supporters of the establishment mainstream. His sudden death, at the age of seventy-eight, in 2005, while addressing a psychical research meeting in London, left the legacy of Scole bereft of one of its most vociferous champions, and was a huge loss to the world of organised psychical research as a whole. Interestingly, Montague Keen is one ghost hunter who seems to have returned on more than one occasion from beyond the grave if recent reports are to be believed. His widow, Veronica Keen, has told me of her experiences at a direct-voice séance held in a private house in Luton a short while after the researcher's death, at which she was convinced her late husband spoke to her through the entranced medium for some time. A personal friend of mine, Janice Fleckney, a natural clairvoyant and developing physical medium from Leighton Buzzard, has also relayed messages seemingly from Keen to his wife during a spiritualist workshop at Cober Hill in Scarborough, organised by medium Melanie Polly in 2005.

For many investigators and paranormal researchers, haunted houses are the real hunting ground for ghosts and supernatural phenomena. A number of Luton's buildings are known to have had haunted reputations over the years, and in the next chapter we will take a look at some of the town's indigenous and interesting phantoms …

three

Haunted Buildings and Houses

PARAPSYCHOLOGISTS and psychical researchers tend to differentiate hauntings into two broad categories: place-centred hauntings, such as the traditional haunted house, and person-centred hauntings, which normally involve some form of poltergeist activity focused on a particular individual or family. Psychically aware people tend to see and experience phenomena in multiple locations, and some cases of haunting can involve both haunting apparitions or ghosts together with the movement of objects and other paranormal activity generally associated with the poltergeist. The English ghost story writer M.R. James (1862-1936) famously stated towards the end of his life that although the existence of ghosts was a certainty, we do not know the rules behind their appearance. This is particularly true where people experience hauntings in newly built or modern houses on sites not known for any previous manifestations or disturbances. There are a number of cases of this type in the Luton area as the following convincing examples clearly show.

In the mid-1970s, the construction firm Laings built a new housing estate on a green-field site overlooking Warden Hill on the north-east outskirts of Luton. A large proportion of these houses, all modern semi-detached dwellings, were treated as an extension of the Old Bedford Road, and Marion Betts and her family have lived there since the estate was finished in 1977. Over a period of several years, their house has been the focus of a protracted haunting, despite being built on farmland and there being no evidence of a former house or building on the site. The most persistent of a number of paranormal incidents reported by the family – which also includes the sound of footsteps and the movement of objects – is the sighting of an apparition seen regularly in the vicinity of the stairs and on the first-floor landing. On a number of occasions, Mrs Betts, while reading in bed with the door open, would be disturbed by the figure of a man dressed in brown monk-like attire, walking up the staircase and across the landing to her bedroom where it would stand for several minutes in the doorway looking into the room; after a time the figure would turn and walk back the way it came and be lost to sight. On another single occasion, Mrs

Betts' son, while in his bedroom and otherwise alone in the house, clearly heard the sound of someone coming up the stairs and along the passageway to his bedroom door; the door handle then moved as though the door were about to be opened, before it returned upright, after which there was silence. On investigation, there was no one outside the room or anywhere else in the house, and all the outside doors were closed and locked.

The most interesting feature of the monkish apparition seen on the staircase is its distinct lack of a face or features: Marion Betts described the figure to me as appearing as though its chin were resting on its chest, as if in an aspect of looking downwards towards the floor, although she acutely felt at the same time she was being observed and that the 'person' was aware of her in the room. This 'faceless' aspect is in fact a common occurrence and appears in many reported sightings of ghosts and apparitions. In some cases the figure is only seen from behind, or, if viewed from the front, the features appear hazy or indistinct, even though the actual body, as well as the arms and legs, are clear and in focus. Sometimes, the apparition seems to purposely obscure its face from being seen. In a famous case, known to psychical researchers as the 'Morton ghost', the apparition of a woman in black, seen frequently for a period of several years during the 1880s in a house (which still stands) in Cheltenham, always hid her features by holding a handkerchief up to the face as if in an attitude of intense grief. Drawing on this and many other instances, it would seem that when people 'see' ghosts, whatever triggers the hallucination of the figure inside the mind of the observer, at times cannot fully conceive or create the impression of a face, the most expressive

and individual part of the human form, although the rest of the figure may be fully realised and appear solid and lifelike. Even when this 'full form' is achieved, there may still be some peculiarities – we recall the appearance of Roy Fulton's phantom hitch-hiker whose face was described as being 'unusually long'. It is easy to see how the many reports of headless ghosts up and down the country (including Luton) stem from this inability for certain apparitions to generate a fully formed face or features, something which gives credence to these kinds of apparition which are very easy to dismiss for being too far-fetched or traditional in nature, i.e. Oscar Wilde's *Canterville Ghost* or Queen Anne Boleyn with their heads under their arms. Rather

Cases of 'faceless' ghosts are often encountered in the history of paranormal research. The famous 'Morton ghost' at Cheltenham in the 1880s was often seen with a handkerchief obscuring its features. (Psychic Press Ltd)

than being the unquiet spirits of beheaded nobility, the appearances of headless figures and apparitions appears to stem from the bizarre and at present seemingly unknowable physics of the paranormal.

The roads and houses forming Luton's Hockwell Ring estate were laid out shortly after the end of the Second World War, although its distinctive tower blocks did not arrive until the mid-1960s. Despite the suburban normality, there are good reasons for considering this to be one of the most haunted parts of Luton. The area is well known for a violent haunting in the late 1970s at Flat 2 in the Green Court tower, involving a young family with a small baby. This case is most often remembered for an exorcism that was carried out after Jennifer Davies and her partner reported experiencing a series of strange and frightening incidents: the baby's cot was shaken as though by an invisible person, household items disappeared and kitchen utensils were thrown about, while the couple claimed to have seen the apparition of (again) a sinister monk-like figure with an badly disfigured face. Following what appears likely to have been a spontaneous fire (a common occurrence in poltergeist hauntings) in the kitchen of their flat, the family felt unable to cope with the escalating and increasingly violent happenings and turned to their local priest, the late Father Don Breen, for help. Breen, a former Vauxhall worker who had come into the priesthood late in life, was a kindly man who was well-liked and respected in the local Catholic community. After meeting with Jennifer Davies he made the decision that an exorcism was the only way to relieve them of their problems and, eschewing official channels, decided to carry out the ceremony himself.

What Father Breen encountered inside the Green Court flat is unclear; although most accounts of the case agree that his involvement brought the haunting to an end, and to date no further disturbances have been reported in this particular building. However, the story of the Hockwell Ring exorcism does not end there, as people who I have discussed the case with who knew Father Don Breen personally, agree that for him the incident had a profound and disturbing effect, both physically and mentally, which lasted several years. After his experience in Green Court, Breen's teachings became 'fire and brimstone', in direct contrast to his previously relaxed presentation of the Catholic liturgy, while the priest himself, formerly a mild-mannered man with a calm persona, seemed troubled and haunted by his experience. Even more startling was the dramatic change to Father Breen's physical appearance: his hair turned white and his skin took on a distinct pale-blue pallor. Chris Harkin, who knew Breen

The Green Court tower block in Luton's Hockwell Ring, scene of a dramatic haunting and exorcism in the late 1970s. (Eddie Brazil)

well, remembered him having to return to Ireland for a period of convalesce shortly after his time in the tower- block flat; after a stay of nearly two years, the priest came back to Luton and his original black hair colour had also returned …

How much coincidence plays in paranormal happenings is difficult to judge. Carol Cyl, who lived in Flat 2 at Green Court for a period of time after the incident of the exorcism, unaware of the flat's previous history, experienced nothing untoward during her time there. However, in another property, a semi-detached house in Hockwell Ring itself, and into which she subsequently moved towards the end of 1989, things were very different, and Carol's experiences form one of the most convincing cases of paranormal phenomena included in this book.

In early 1991, around a year after they had moved into the house, Carol Cyl noticed that her three-year-old daughter Laurie had gained an imaginary playmate that was brightening up her usual bath times. Satisfied that the young child was safe enough to be left in the bath while she quickly folded clothes and tidied up her bedroom, Carol became increasingly intrigued by the regular and happy sounds of laughter as well as talking as Laurie amused herself while her mother was out of the room. When questioned, her daughter confided that her new friend, called Beatrice, only played with her when Carol was away from the bathroom; when her mother came back, Beatrices would go and only return when Laurie was alone again. Something about her description of her bath-time friend made Carol inclined to believe that there was something more involved than Laurie's active and playfully innocent imagination. Beatrice was always a very dirty little girl who *came through the wall* when Carol was out of the room, and

quickly disappeared in the same eerie way; and it wasn't long before Carol Cyl saw a ghost in the same house herself.

Around a fortnight after her daughter had described her playmate Beatrice, the young mother found herself suddenly awake in the middle of the night. The house was dark and silent and, looking across to the bedside table, she saw the digital clock flick over at that exact moment to midnight. Immediately, Carol became aware of a heavy stifling feeling, almost akin to suffocation, which had seemingly woken her, almost as though the house was on fire and smoke was filling the room. As she looked across to the open bedroom door, she saw the figure of an old man with a heavily wisened face, wearing what appeared to be a night cap and gown, who stood silently, staring at her intently. The apparition appeared solid and lifelike, although it was surrounded by what could be described as a hazy glow or 'aura'. Transfixed by the presence of the figure, Carol watched, terrified, for several minutes until the old man began to fade away, reducing from the outside inwards until it had completely disappeared. The face with its piercing eyes was the last part of the apparition to vanish, and Carol spent the rest of the night awake with the bedroom light on.

During their time at Hockwell Ring, the family also experienced several instances of physical phenomena inside the house. Regularly, kitchen-cupboard doors as well as the kitchen window would often be found open when all in the house were adamant that they had been left closed. The most startling incident occurred sometime during the night following a party after several guests had left and the family had finally gone to bed. A half-pint glass, half-full with beer, which had been left on a sideboard, was discovered the follow-

An ordinary house in Hockwell Ring, where the apparitions of a young girl and a man with staring eyes were seen in the early 1990s. (Eddie Brazil).

ing morning to have shattered in a bizarre manner. The top half of the glass down to the contents had broken into tiny fragments which were scattered over the surface of the sideboard, and the line of the broken edge was perfectly level with the surface of the beer. No one had been downstairs and the manner of the breaking of the glass itself seemed almost physically impossible, something that psychical researchers with experience of investigating poltergeist cases often report as taking place regularly during hauntings of this nature. Sometime later, after Carol Cyl had moved out of the house, she had cause to speak with the previous tenant who also admitted to having experienced the haunting herself. On several occasions her twin sons complained to their mother that during the night two small boys would come into their bedroom and silently sit at the end of their beds watching them …

During the early 2000s, residents in another house in Hockwell Ring, this time in Brickly Road and only a short walk from both Carol Cyl's house and the Green Court tower, experienced a number of startling and inexplicable manifestations. Charlie Harkin, who lived in the house for a time, has described hearing footsteps walking about in the first-floor rooms while he and a friend, the only tenants at the time, sat downstairs watching television. On one occasion, clothes drying on a clothes horse in one of the bedrooms were found the next morning neatly placed over the surface of the duvet cover – this had taken place during the night while the occupant of the room was asleep and undisturbed. Another tenant claimed to have seen the apparition of an old man in the house a number of times, although the most frightening incident involved a young female visitor who became hysterical after claiming to have seen a dead man sitting in an armchair in the living room. Interestingly, it was later found that a previous occupant *had* been discovered dead in a chair in the same room twelve years previously. Another girl also became extremely distressed, claiming that an unseen person blew on her face at night in an empty bedroom.

A number of cases in this book involve encounters with phantom children, and child ghosts are frequently reported in many hauntings across the country. On the south side of Luton, the Luton and Dunstable Hospital's Children's Annexe stood for many years in Tennyson Road, on a plot of land adjacent to what is now the Tennyson Road Primary School. The annexe buildings have now been demolished and a new housing estate occupies the site. One particular house appears to contain echoes from the past as I have collected an account of the apparition of a little girl, around six years of age, who

St Margaret's church at Streatley, north of Luton. The churchyard is said to be haunted by the ghost of a former rector, the Revd James Hadow. (Eddie Brazil)

was seen quite regularly there at one time. On one occasion, following a children's party, a helium balloon which had been left floating against the ceiling in the living room, was seen to move by itself as though being dragged along by an invisible hand holding onto the trailing string. The doors and windows in the room were closed at the time and the jerky movement of the balloon was exactly as one would expect it to appear as it was pulled along by a child at play.

Child ghosts have also been suggested as the cause of paranormal disturbances at a modern factory in (appropriately enough)

Cemetery Road, Houghton Regis, which took place over a period of several months during 2009. The factory floor in what was and still is an engineering works was disturbed on a regular basis, particularly at night, and a first-floor office area was also affected. Several people reported hearing footsteps, objects were moved and, on occasion, thrown about, and several of the staff became reluctant to spend time in the building on their own. One incident, which took place during the day, involved the paranormal movement of a cardboard box which was being packed with completed machine parts. Gary Courtney (pseudonym), who was working in a part of the factory on his own preparing components for delivery, described placing items inside an ordinary shipping box, briefly turning away to pick up some labels from a nearby bench and, on turning round, discovering that the box and its contents had moved 4ft along the counter, seemingly by themselves. Workers also described feeling a presence when alone in the upstairs office suite. Jan Fleckney, who visited the factory in the company of two fellow clairvoyants, described to me her impressions of a number of child 'entities' that she picked up as being present in the building and who, mischievously, were causing much of the disturbances.

From newly recorded and obscure cases we move to look at some of Luton's more well-known hauntings. Churches, chapels and abbeys can be a rich hunting ground for the ghost hunter as many of these ecclesiastical buildings have long, and at times, violent histories. Two hauntings associated with the Luton area are unfortunately somewhat anecdotal in nature, but interesting nonetheless. The churches within Luton itself appear to have no haunted histories, but a mile-and-a-half to the north at Streatley, the ghost of a former rector, the Revd James Hadow, is said to walk in the churchyard of the early thirteenth-century St Margaret's. The church was rescued from dereliction in the 1930s and reopened in October 1938 by the then Bishop of St Albans, Dr Michael Furse. When and by whom the spectre of Hadow has been seen is not known, but the story is a persistent one and perhaps has some basis in fact. A well-known but again anecdotal haunting is that of the imposing

The interior of the Priory Church of St Peter, Dunstable, where the ghost of Cuthbert, the second prior, is said to visit the choir stalls at night. (Eddie Brazil)

Church of St Peter, formerly the church of the Augustinian Priory of Dunstable. St Peter's ghosts are Cuthbert, the second prior, who is said to visit the choir stalls at night, and more famously a local character, a wise woman known as Sally the Witch, whose troublesome spirit was allegedly caught in a glass bottle and buried at an unknown spot in the churchyard. This colourful story has been researched by Luton ghost hunter William King, while Damien O'Dell has looked closely into the history of St Peter's, and both researchers have published their findings.

The streetscapes and skyline of Luton town centre have undergone extensive change in the years following the Second World War, particularly during the 1960s and 1970s with the construction of dual-carriageway roads, such as the Chapel Street and Park Street viaducts, numerous office blocks, and the arrival of the mighty Arndale Shopping Centre; all of which have removed former landmarks and reduced the physical structures of local history to dim and distant memories. In the first half of the twentieth century, entertainment in Luton was provided by several cinemas, as well as two impressive local theatres. The Grand, the county's first purpose-built theatre, opened by Lillie Langtry in December 1898, was a much loved local venue for over fifty years before closing in 1957. The building was demolished soon after and today it is all but forgotten, its old site obliterated by the building of the Arndale in the early 1970s. Theatres are well known as haunted places. The 'Man in Grey', seen many times over the years at Drury Lane Theatre, is one of London's most famous ghosts, while the French writer Gaston Leroux (1868-1927) clearly went a long way in reinforcing the sinister side of theatre buildings in the public consciousness with the publication of his 1910 novel, *The Phantom of the Opera*. If the Grand Theatre was a haunted building then records of its ghosts have not survived. However, the Grand's rival, the Alma, which first opened for business on 21 December 1929, was a haunted building, with a history of many strange happenings.

The Alma Kinema, purpose-built for the 'talkies', occupied a prominent corner site at the junction of Alma Street and Manchester Street. Designed as a cine-variety hall, it had a chequered and somewhat convoluted history. In its original form its auditorium held over 1,600 people; films were shown on an impressive Magnascope wide-screen, and there was a Compton organ for music recitals, a stage for live theatre, as well as a small ballroom and a tea lounge. During the war years, the

Luton's Alma Theatre photographed in the early 1950s. Stories of a curse, an unseen presence and ghostly footsteps were well known here during the first half of the twentieth century. (Bedfordshire and Luton Archives Service)

The Cresta House office block which now stands on the site of the former haunted Alma Theatre. (Eddie Brazil)

Alma changed to a full-time variety hall (when it was known simply as the Alma Theatre) but began showing films again at the beginning of 1944. Four years later, the Alma lost its cinema screen and changed again to become a full-time live theatre. The theatre's final performance was given on 17 July 1954, after which the building closed and was converted into a ballroom, known as the Alma Ballroom and later, the Cresta, before finally shutting for good in May 1960. It was later demolished, a Herculean task given the size of the

building, which sent the first contractor into bankruptcy before a second successfully completed the job, and the Cresta House office block now occupies the site.

The stars of the day, including Maurice Chevalier, Elsie and Doris Waters, Hughie Green, Derek Roy, Julie Andrews and Dick Emery, trod the boards at the Alma Theatre. In 1951, Hollywood legend Bela Lugosi, gave twelve performances of a stage production of *Dracula*, the role which had made him famous as a cinema horror actor twenty years before in director

Tod Browning's landmark cinema version. Eric Lindsay, who played the lunatic Renfield in the production, recounted his time at the Alma to Lugosi historian, Andi Brooks, specifically in connection with the theatre's paranormal reputation:

I cannot recall anything strange or ghostly about the Alma Theatre, Luton. Luton is a strange place anyway; in fact if there were ghosts in the theatre we could have done with them to sit in the audience and liven up the proceedings! As far as I recall, audiences were not responsive – in fact they were deadly.

Lindsay may not have encountered anything paranormal during his brief stay in Luton, but a number of people who worked there during its various incarnations over the years have claimed that the Alma was both a haunted and a cursed building.

Tony Broughall, who played in jazz bands at the Alma on a number of occasions, remembers much of the local reputation the complex held for most of the time it was standing:

Before the first brick was laid, the Alma appeared to run into trouble of a supernatural nature. The site had been

Newspaper advert for the 1951 stage production of Dracula at Luton's Alma Theatre, starring master of the macabre, Bela Lugosi, in the title role. (Andi Brooks)

occupied by terraced houses and cottages which were sold over the heads of the tenants, thus forcing them to find alternative accommodation. The anger and resentment this caused led to talk of a curse being placed on the site of the new building. Who placed the curse is not known but it was certainly widely talked about at the time and gained some credibility when a workman was killed during the Alma's construction. There are two versions of the story, one being that he was drunk when he fell from the roof girders into the partially completed circle, the other that he was accidentally knocked off his balance by another workman. Whatever the merits of either story, an old cap, heavily encrusted with what could have been bloodstains, was found in the circle girder-work during the demolition of the building in 1961.

Putting the Alma 'curse' aside, it would seem a number of people employed at the theatre reported experiencing unusual things, such as an atmosphere of unease which seemed to fill the backstage areas of the building, and an unseen presence that followed staff members up and down both of the two internal service staircases, together with frightening sensations of being pushed from behind. Harold Hall, the Alma's musical director during the early 1950s, refused to work in a particular room after staying late one night to prepare a score for a forthcoming performance, and quit the theatre shortly afterwards. No satisfactory reason was given for his resignation, and he avoided discussing why he found his former office so unpleasant. Today it is impossible to say where this 'haunting' had its origins. If the old houses that were cleared away to make way for its construction were known for similar happenings

then records or accounts have not survived. The Alma Theatre remains a classic but ultimately enigmatic Luton haunting.

Directly opposite the site of the old Alma and built on what was at one time the former Crown and Anchor brewery, is its modern equivalent, the Galaxy entertainment centre, which includes a multi-screen cinema and bowling alley, together with several eateries and restaurants. This building, which opened to the public in October 1998, may possibly, due to such close proximity with its haunted predecessor, have inherited something of the Alma's former otherworldliness, although local ghost hunter William King has suggested that the brewery site was known for ghostly stories long before the site was redeveloped. The Cineworld section of the building has garnered a reputation for being haunted, in particular Screen 6 where staff members have seen what has been described as a black shadowy figure, and heard unusual noises; sensations of extreme coldness have also been reported. Whether the Galaxy is a new building with the remnants of an old haunting remains to be seen, and to date no organised investigation by ghost hunting groups has been carried out here. The site has seen much physical change over the years: the brewery was replaced by a Co-Op store which was damaged by fire and subsequently demolished after standing empty and derelict, after which the land was used as a car park before work on the Galaxy began. It would seem likely that the paranormal activity reported in the area of Screen 6 is a new haunting, the origins of which, like that of ghostly activity in general, remains obscure.

Feelings of intense coldness – together with the sound of footsteps – are one of the most widely reported phenomena

The modern Galaxy entertainment centre in St George's Square, where cinema employees have experienced unusual phenomena including mysterious 'cold spots', noises and the appearance of a black shadowy figure. (Eddie Brazil)

reported by visitors to haunted buildings. They can be both short-term 'cold spots' or form an almost permanent background to a haunted area. A work colleague of mine, David Beynon, the former Chief Architect of Benskins Brewery, worked during the 1950s in a period building at No.4 Berkeley Street, Mayfair, itself a stone's throw from the Ritz in London. His office was a small room on the second floor which, despite a large old-fashioned radiator, was constantly cold, even during the height of summer. When this was mentioned casually in passing to another member of staff, David was told that during the Second World War, an officer on leave had jumped to his death from the window of the room into the street below, rather than return to his regiment.

Another modern Luton town-centre building which has obtained paranormal connections in recent years is the BBC Three Counties Radio headquarters situated on the corner of Hastings Street and Regent Street. In 2004, staff members reported a number of unusual incidents, most notably the sighting of the apparition of a blonde woman, described as being in her early forties and wearing a dress and hat, who was seen standing in the first-floor reception area on two occasions; when a BBC receptionist went to speak to her (which involved leaving her desk and walking around a glass screen) the figure had disappeared. The paranormality of the unknown woman appeared to be strengthened by the fact that access to the reception area at the time could only be achieved by a buzzer and door-lock system; on each occasion that the figure was seen, no one had either let anyone into the reception or opened the door for them to leave, and anyone leaving in the normal way would have been observed in the time that it took for the receptionist to leave her desk and walk into the public area,. Interestingly, the figure was described as appearing 'with her head cast down' in the same way, as we have previously seen, that is common with the appearance of certain types of apparition. An account of a contemporary investigation of the Three Counties building, carried out at the time of the disturbances, by the Anglia Paranormal Investigation Society, is given by Damien O'Dell, (who we will encounter again in a later chapter) in *Paranormal Bedfordshire* (2008).

A site that appears to have at least two resident ghosts is the former Skefko Ball Bearing Co. works in Leagrave Road, now known as Britannia House. The Skefko company was founded in Gothenburg, Sweden and construction of their purpose-built factory was begun in 1910;

The BBC Three Counties Radio building on the corner of Regent Street and Hastings Street, scene of strange happenings during the mid-2000s. (Eddie Brazil)

production commenced in June the following year and by the 1920s, Skefko was one of Luton's biggest employers with over 1,000 staff. The company eventually expanded to a second site, two-and-a-half miles away in Sundon. During the 1960s the Leagrave plant was gradually wound down and production transferred to this sister plant, a process which was completed in 1977, and from where SKF (UK) Ltd still operates today. In 1972, canteen staff at the Leagrave Road factory claimed to have had several encounters with the apparition of a former female worker who had died in 1963 under tragic circumstances and who had been employed at the plant for over twenty-five years. Two Luton women, Dora Rouget and Tina Tyrrell, both saw a woman dressed in white boots and overalls who appeared solid and lifelike, and who they initially mistook for another member of staff. On both occasions, the figure disappeared in such a way that was impossible for a living person to effect. As she was washing her hands in the restroom, Mrs Tyrrell clearly saw the person pass by her and enter a cloakroom immediately adjacent; when she went and looked inside, the cloakroom was empty – no one had left and there was no other way out of the room. Both workers were understandably shaken and upset by their experiences. After this initial flurry of activity, the canteen haunting appears to have petered out and by the time SKF closed its doors in Leagrave Road, no further sightings of the ghost had been reported. In recent years, however, another apparition appears to have become active here. In May 2005, an unnamed female employee at the Britannia Estate contacted the *Luton News* claiming to have encountered the ghost of an old man with white hair and unusually long finger nails while working alone in the building, which has now been converted into multiple-occupancy business suites. The figure spoke and described being an employee at the Skefko works in the past. How many other people have had similar experiences is not clear, but this second ghost at the former Leagrave Road factory seems to have been seen on the premises more than once.

It is worth rounding off this section of our ghost tour with two Dunstable hauntings which again demonstrate the great disparity between the different types of haunted building encountered by psychical researchers across the country. The strange story of No. 49 Edward Street, Dunstable is a forgotten haunting waiting to be rediscovered. A mid-terraced Victorian property, the original No. 49 dated from the mid-1850s and was demolished in the late 1980s. It was reconstructed as an example of modern urban infill, replacing the existing building with a development of four flats built in a style matching that of the existing, while at the same time the old garden, where five deep wells were known to exist, was turned into a car park. The old house had a mysterious haunted history stretching back many years. Before the building was converted into two flats in the mid-1960s, the figure of a woman was often seen standing at the top of the stairs, and on studying the case it becomes clear that the upper floor was in fact the most haunted part of the house.

In November 1965, the Haywood family, young newlyweds with a baby, moved into the first-floor flat. Four months later, Val Haywood saw the apparition of 'a man with grey hair and dressed in old-fashioned clothes' standing in one of the bedrooms. The family dog also became aware of the supernatural presence and as well as refusing to enter the room where the ghost was seen,

The former Skefko Ball Bearing Co. building in Leagrave Road, now known as Britannia House. Reports of apparitions here began to circulate in the early 1970s. (Eddie Brazil)

ran away from the house on three occasions. Not long after, the ground-floor flat became vacant and Mrs Haywood, upset by her experience, persuaded her husband to move downstairs. At the same time, another couple, Christine Ayles and her husband, who were friends of the Haywoods and in need of immediate accommodation, expressed an interest in the first-floor flat of No. 49 Edward Street, and in March 1966 they moved in, unaware of the supernatural experiences of their predecessors. Later the same month, the ghosts returned. Christine Ayles awoke to find the figure of a woman in Edwardian clothes wearing a round hat standing at the foot of her bed, looking at her intently. On waking her husband she found that the woman had disappeared. The following month, while alone in her flat, Mrs Haywood, who knew her upstairs neighbour was out, heard the footsteps of someone walking around the floor above.

Two views of the original house at No. 49 Edward Street, Dunstable, the scene of much paranormal activity over many years. *(Tony Broughall/Peter Underwood Collection)*

The Chrysler UK truck factory office block at Boscombe Road, Dunstable, now demolished, where Luton ghost hunter Tony Broughall investigated the ghost of a former worker. (Paul Adams)

On her return, Mrs Ayles confirmed that she had found the flat exactly as she had left it and the outside door and windows were closed.

Four days later, at around 4 p.m., Christine Ayles went to go into a spare bedroom at the back of the house and was immediately confronted by the apparition of the grey-haired man in black that had so upset her neighbour the previous month. The figure had his back to her, and the young housewife, now very scared by what was happening, immediately ran downstairs where she thankfully found Val Haywood working in her kitchen. On looking up to the back of the house from the kitchen window, they each saw the man in side-profile through the spare-bedroom window. This experience was enough for both women and they and their families subsequently moved out.

The origins of the Edward Street ghosts are obscure and it is a case that would benefit from further historical investigation.

In 2010, a neighbour described to me a number of incidents that had taken place during the 1980s, by which time both flats were vacant and the building was in a semi-derelict condition. Despite the electricity supply having been cut off at the meter, the local police were called on a number of occasions to investigate reports of the room lights switching on and off, seemingly by themselves. No break-ins were ever found and officers confirmed that there was no power at all throughout the house.

A final haunting proves that ghosts can be found in the most unlikely of places, as during the 1970s, a working truck factory in Boscombe Road, Dunstable, was to provide ghost-buster Tony Broughall with one of his most interesting and convincing cases. Now recently demolished and the site cleared for redevelopment, the former office building associated with Chrysler's UK truck division, then recently constructed in 1968, became the focus for unusual happenings in 1970 when several office workers became convinced that they were being haunted by the ghost of a deceased colleague. As well as the sound of footsteps, doors opening and closing, together with sensations of sudden coldness and lights switching on and off, a number of people, including a security guard and two cleaners, reported seeing the apparition of a middle-aged man wearing a dark blue pin-striped suit several times inside the building. On one occasion, the figure, seemingly solid and lifelike, was seen collectively by four people sitting at a desk; when approached, the apparition suddenly vanished when a cleaner was within 8ft of where the person was sitting. In 1975, Tony Broughall, at that time a Chrysler employee at the Boscombe Road plant, was able to interview a number of witnesses who claimed to have experienced phenomena as well as naming the person whose ghost appeared to have haunted the building five years before. After carrying out a thorough investigation, it seemed to the researcher an almost inescapable fact that for a period of several months in what was a plain and ordinary run-of-the-mill office, a dead man had come back to work …

four

Haunted Pubs and Hostelries

UBLIC houses and inns have been traditional meeting places providing shelter and company, as well as staging posts for travellers, for centuries, so it is no surprise that these buildings and their environs are some of the most commonly haunted buildings in the country. Ghosts appear in the oldest hostelries as well as in the newest. The Bingley Arms in the picturesque Yorkshire village of Bardsey is considered to be the oldest inn in England with a known history dating back to at least AD 953. Its ghosts include a phantom dog as well as the apparitions of a young woman and a Cavalier wearing a large-brimmed hat. In the mid-1990s, I met an architect involved in converting a former 1930s cinema in London into a new Wetherspoons pub, who told me that workmen on the site were refusing to go into one area of the building after one of the contractors claimed to have seen a headless figure in what had originally been the old projection room. Many of Bedfordshire's pubs have ghostly associations and here we will spend some time looking at the haunted histories of a number of Luton and Dunstable hostelries.

Henry I established a hunting lodge in Dunstable early in the twelfth century on a nine-acre site on the north side of what is now Church Street, directly opposite the haunted Church of St Peter that we have already visited. A hundred years later the lodge, known as Kingsbury, was given to the priory by King John, brother of Richard the Lionheart, and the monks soon leased the buildings to local wool merchants. The site was developed as Kingsbury Farm by the Marsh family – William Marsh, a farmer with estates in nearby Caddington and Kensworth, had bought the land in the early 1600s. The buildings on the site today date from the late eighteenth century. In the early 1960s, the estate was split up and sold off, with one part becoming a handsome private house known as Kingsbury Court, in the former grounds of which, now redeveloped into flats, Tony Broughall has collected an account of an alleged haunted lavatory. The other buildings are known as the Old Palace Hotel, while a former barn, which had at one time been used as the Dunstable Museum, was converted by the Flowers Brewery into a public house and opened as the Norman King in 1961.

Some unseen aspect of the building's former days or occupants seemed at times to return to the Norman King as over the years it gained a reputation for a persistent but gentle haunting. The areas of the building most affected were the dining restaurant and the adjacent kitchen where objects were found unaccountably moved and where doors often appeared to open and close by themselves. Much of this activity, which also included interference with cooking equipment, refrigerators, as well as beer engines in the tap room, was put down to the mischievous ghost of a little boy who was allegedly seen on one occasion by the young daughter of a member of staff. In the early hours of the morning of 10 August 2011, the Norman King pub was destroyed by fire in an arson attack and the burnt-out ruins, unsafe and beyond repair, were subsequently demolished. Whether the ghost or ghosts of this landmark Dunstable hostelry will ever be experienced again remains to be seen. At the time of writing (January 2012), the site adjacent to the Old Palace Hotel remains derelict.

Another Dunstable building with a haunted history now no longer standing is the Brewery House, which occupied a corner site at the junction of High Street North and Chiltern Road before being demolished in 1974. By the 1960s, this former brewery had been converted into

The Norman King public house in Dunstable, allegedly haunted by the ghost of a young child. The building was destroyed by fire in 2011. (National Education Network)

flats, but the site was known locally to have had an unhappy history. A number of murders and several suicides are alleged to have taken place in the past, so perhaps it was not surprising that in August 1967, the *Dunstable Gazette* received a report that the apparition of a young woman had been seen in the building by one of the tenants. Mr and Mrs Sweetman claimed to have experienced poltergeist-like phenomena while the ghost itself appeared to Mrs Sweetman in her bedroom as a hazy grey figure. The couple were apparently so unnerved that they slept on a mattress on the living-room floor rather than stay for any length of time in the haunted room, and subsequently fled the flat in such a hurry that they left behind all of their furniture and personal possessions. The Sweetman's rapid departure was confirmed to the newspaper by Brian Sweetman's mother. Despite a clergyman being asked to perform an exorcism by one of the tenants, neighbours in the same building were less inclined to believe in a paranormal explanation for the couple's absence, with the result that today the real facts behind the haunting of the Brewery House remain something of a mystery. The site was later redeveloped and a new public house, the Chiltern, built on the old brewery grounds. Later renamed the Priory Pub & Restaurant, this is now closed and empty so, to paraphrase the ghosts of American novelist Shirley Jackson's *Hill House*, whatever walks the site of the Brewery House today, walks there alone …

Haunted Houghton Regis has provided a number of good cases for the present book and the Old Red Lion, a seventeenth-century Grade II listed building in Bedford Road, adds a hostelry with supernatural connections to our survey.

This somewhat homely haunting dates from the early 1980s when the then licensees, Harvey and Doreen May, attributed a regular series of inexplicable incidents to a resident phantom known as both 'Fred' and 'Freda'. The couple often found ornaments had been moved around the public bars during the night; on one occasion cigarette butts from an ashtray were discovered under Harvey May's pillow. A hanging sign over the bar counter would often begin to swing on its own, as if being moved by an invisible hand, while an incident that took place during the time a relief couple were managing the pub when an amount of money which went missing, presumed stolen but later found in the office safe, was put down to the activities of the ghostly 'Fred'. A smell of perfume 'in unusual places' around the pub was also considered another aspect of the ghost's activities, and one which gave rise to the notion of 'a Freda ghost' haunting the building, which, according to local tradition, is thought to have been built on the site of a holy well. During the time the Mays were resident at the Old Red Lion, the premises underwent a £40,000 refurbishment which appears to have affected the psychic fabric as well as the physical structure as, paranormally, this public house, now a Crown Carvery, appears quiet today.

Violent tragedy is often considered the root cause of ghostly activity in haunted buildings up and down the country. An incident which took place at the Four Horse Shoes in Park Street, Luton, in 1908, when the landlord, William Littlewood Clifford, was burnt to death, has been linked to reports of unusual noises being heard on occasion by bar staff, akin to the sounds of money being counted, and is an example of this type of case. In the early hours of the morning of 31 July, a fire broke out in the ground-floor tap room which soon spread to the upper parts of the building. Mr Clifford closed the premises promptly at 11.00 p.m. and retired with his wife to their small bedroom situated over the bar. The landlord's nephew, as well as two male lodgers, were also asleep in other parts of the building. The *Luton News* for 6 August 1908 describes the deadly drama which unfolded a short time later:

During the dark hours of the night, the police patrolling the street found nothing that awakened the slightest suspicion. The lamp-lighter for the district, who is a fireman, also saw nothing of the fire that, all the time, must have been smouldering in the bar, as he passed the house on his round about 2.30 a.m. Barely an hour after, however, the landlord was aroused by flames that, in an ever-increasing volume, were finding their way upstairs. Instantly, the household was roused, but, under-estimating the seriousness of the fire raging below, Mr Clifford went down the cramped, match-boarded staircase … As soon as he opened the door to the sitting-room, just behind the front bar, and saw what a hold the fire had obtained, he must, however, have realised his position. But, for some reason unknown he elected to go on. Thinking, possibly, that it was his duty, for the sake of those still above, to find his way out of the house and raise an alarm, he rushed through the sitting room to the side door. What followed can only be surmised. The outlet that he had created by opening the sitting-room door probably caused a sudden rush of fumes and flames, and, though he reached the side door, as shown by the position in which his charred body was found, he never succeeded in opening it.

Whilst this grim tragedy was being enacted below, the lodgers sleeping in the gable bedroom, found that escape by the staircase was impossible, and let themselves down into the yard with the bedclothes. Mrs Clifford, her nephew, and a dog which usually slept upstairs, made their way, at the same time, into the sitting room over the front bar and called for help. It was then 3.40 a.m. Fortunately, P.C. Harbord, who was on duty in the Park Street district, heard the cries of 'fire'. Running into the middle of the road, opposite Chobham Street, he at once saw the Four Horse Shoes burst into flames. Blowing his whistle, he ran at once to the scene. By that time, the lodgers, unmindful of the probable loss of their own clothing, had carried a ladder, found in the yard, to the front of the house. The landlord's little nephew was immediately rescued, but it was with great difficulty that P.C. Harbord succeeded in bringing Mrs Clifford from her perilous position to the ground.

It has been surmised by some that William Clifford lost his life in a desperate attempt to rescue a cash box from the tap room which contained the takings from the previous evening. It is not surprising then, that the ghostly noises in today's Four Horse Shoes, now renamed simply the Horseshoes, have been linked to his unquiet spirit which may still hold a presence over his former home and business.

Other Luton pubs are reputed to have ghostly associations. The Cork & Bull, a short walk from the old Four Horse Shoes in adjoining Cumberland Street, is the haunt of a white lady apparition named Ann, said to be the ghost of a former elderly resident who was murdered on the premises and who now returns

The Four Horse Shoes public house, said to be haunted by the ghost of a former landlord, William Clifford, who was burnt to death during a fire on the premises in 1908. (Eddie Brazil)

periodically, moving and throwing objects as well as materialising in various locations, both inside the building as well as in the roadway outside. In July 2007, the Luton Paranormal Society headed to the Biscot Mill, a 1950s road pub built on the site of a working smock mill which was pulled down in the 1930s, following reports of unusual activity inside the building. Evidence exists for a windmill on the site going back at least into the latter part of the seventeenth century, while a sure-fire catalyst for the creation of ghostly stories in the neighbourhood took place during the 1920s when a Saxon cemetery containing evidence of many burials and extending from Argyll Avenue to the south-east up the hill, possibly to the immediate area of the Biscot Mill, was discovered by two local Luton historians.

However, Luton's premier inn for convincing evidence of paranormal activity must be the Moat House in the former village (now a suburb) of Limbury, two miles north-west of the town centre.

The oldest building on the Moat House site dates from the closing decades of the fourteenth century when most likely the de Bereford family constructed a moated and thatched residential hall complete with courtyard, kitchens and stabling. Another local family, the Ackworths, had a long association with the site, from 1400 through until the mid-1500s. The building has seen much alteration and additions down through the years. At the beginning of the sixteenth century the original hall was re-roofed, and by the start of the 1600s the building had been divided up into a series of smaller rooms. An iconic record of these times exists in the form of an inscribed stone plaque, formerly located in the cellar of the building, which records that on 23 July 1666, the year of the Great Fire of London, hailstones the size of pebbles fell during a storm around the house. The building underwent extensive modernisation towards the end of the Swinging Sixties and today is a well frequented local hostelry with a popular daily carvery. Interestingly, and perhaps of no surprise due to its extensive age and history, the Moat House is known to paranormal researchers for its psychic activity as much as for the quality of its food and drink.

The most persistently reported phenomenon that has come out of the Moat House over several years is the sighting of the apparition of a figure in white, invariably described as being a veiled woman, which has been seen in the building, both in the older sections as well as the modern additions. A common belief is that the ghost is that of a former nun who lived in a convent which once occupied a tract of land close by, and the name of the road where the Moat House stands, Nunnery Lane, together with the apparent veiling or headdress seen on the figure, would appear to support this theory. There are, however, problems with the idea of a ghostly nun in this part of Luton, and the case of the ghost nun of Limbury draws parallels with a similar apparition, the famous phantom nun associated with the 'most haunted house in England', Borley Rectory, located fifty miles away in rural Essex. At Borley, a local tradition that the haunted rectory had been built on the site of a former monastery, and that one of the monks there had been involved

The Moat House at Limbury. Ghostly phenomena reported here include lights being switched on and off, together with the apparition of a veiled woman in white. (Eddie Brazil)

in a clandestine affair with a nun from the nearby convent at Bures, seemed to provide an explanation for the appearance of apparitions seen in the rectory grounds over what amounts to a period of many years. This tradition was exposed as being nothing more than a legend by psychical researchers in the 1930s and, as at Borley, there is no evidence that a religious order ever in fact existed at either Limbury, or nearby Biscot, in the past. In the case of the Moat House, it is possible to see where the errors have been made and where the idea of a ghostly nun has its origins.

In 1855, William Davis, a Luton shoe-maker, published his thirteen-part *The History of Luton, with its Hamlets, Etc.* which contained reference to, 'a consider-able house for Nuns, founded by Roger, Abbot of St Albans, and dedicated to the Holy Trinity'. This convent was located at Limbury-cum-Biscot, and at the time of the Dissolution of the Monasteries in 1538 it was valued at £143 18s 3d. In the late 1920s, when Luton Council under-took a programme of naming several new roads throughout the town, this religious link with the area was honoured in the naming of Nunnery Lane, which was rati-fied at a council meeting on 13 December 1928. Unfortunately, William Davis had got his facts wrong and had confused Biscot in Luton with the nunnery at Markyate Cell, a place we have already encountered in con-nection with the ghostly Katherine Ferrers. Luton historian William Austin noticed

the mistake and included an account in his own *The History of Luton and Its Hamlets*, a two-volume work that was published posthumously in 1928. Austin had died earlier the same year, the same time that also saw the erroneous naming of Nunnery Lane before his corrections were made public.

The Moat House haunting may not involve a phantom nun, but there is no doubting the fact that strange and unusual happenings have taken place in what is the oldest secular building in Luton on a regular basis, most notably the sighting of a nun-like apparition. As recently as 2010, an assistant manager at the pub claimed to have seen the figure of a woman dressed in white clothing standing at the far end of the main dining room in what would have been the courtyard of the origi-nal Moat House farm late one night. The incident was unsettling enough to cause her to be signed-off sick from work for several weeks. Lynne McGoghegan, who worked for some time as a cleaner at the Moat House, has described to me a number of inexplicable incidents that took place while she was working on the premises, including the turning on and off of lights in parts of the building known to have been empty at the time, as well as a glimpse of a figure which walked past her and clearly went down the stairs into the cellar area; on immediate inspection, the beer cellar, from which the staircase is the only exit, was completely empty …

five

Hills, Parks and Open Spaces

THE next part of our survey of Luton's paranormal heritage moves away from the town's built up areas to focus on a number of local undeveloped sites that again have connections with the strange and intriguing world of the unseen. As it does it brings into play a collection of reported encounters that seem to combine traditional hauntings with other darker aspects of the supernatural world, specifically Satanism, witchcraft and Fortean phenomena such as cryptozoology and the existence of legendary creatures. In the fast-moving technology-obsessed Britain of today, these subjects would seem to some impossible and also slightly absurd. However, past events can cast long shadows down through the years and perhaps it is unsettling for the sceptics to learn that all of the incidents included in this chapter have their basis in solid facts.

The winter of 1962-63 is remembered as not only being the harshest of the twentieth century but one of the coldest winter periods for the United Kingdom since temperature records began to be kept around the middle of the 1600s. For many people snow began falling on Boxing Day and plummeting temperatures together with severe blizzards ensured it still lay frozen on the ground over two months later. At Herne Bay in Kent the sea froze for over a mile out from the shoreline, two thousand ponies were buried under drifts on Dartmoor, there were several deaths attributed to the Arctic conditions and as well as severe power failures, the railway system fell into chaos. It was not until the beginning of March 1963 that the country experienced its first night without frost; on 6 March, London enjoyed its warmest day since the end of the previous October and soon rising temperatures cleared the remaining snow after more than eleven long and difficult weeks.

Lutonians accustomed to reading endless accounts of the bad weather in the local newspapers were no doubt surprised and shocked to see the headlines on the front page of the *Luton News* for 21 March 1963 when these problems were put temporarily to one side by a sensational report of vandalism and desecrations at an abandoned fifteenth-century church at Clophill, twelve miles to the north on the A6, a village already associated in the public eye with the macabre

The ruins of St Mary's Old Church at Clophill. Known as the 'Black Magic church', the site has a sinister history of Satanic worship, desecration, vandalism and haunting going back fifty years. (Eddie Brazil)

due to the then recent 1961 Hanratty shooting. 'Voodooism Or Vandalism?: Clophill Folk Blame Grave Robbers' was the title of a lengthy illustrated article by staff reporter Brian Swain, who described the discovery by two Luton schoolboys of the bones of Jenny Humberstone, the wife of a former village apothecary, who had died in 1770 at the age of twenty-two. Parts of her skeleton had been removed from their grave and arranged inside the ruined hilltop church in such a way that seemingly implied some kind of Satanic or Black Magic ritual. Soon occultists, ghost hunters and sensation-seekers were beating a path to Clophill village and the incident proved to be the catalyst that has given the old church of St Mary's a sinister haunted reputation which survives unabated to this day.

A number of researchers have been drawn to the Clophill story. Folklore and witchcraft expert Eric Maple included the case in a number of books and lectures, ghost hunter Damien O'Dell has covered the haunted angle in his *Paranormal Bedfordshire* (2008), and there is a concise summary of the Clophill affair in my own *Shadows in the Nave* (2011). The most detailed investigation has been carried out by Hertfordshire-based film-maker Kevin Gates whose researches have brought to light a little known but nonetheless strange and disturbing connection with the 'Black Magic' church of Clophill that is much closer to home than a lot of present-day Luton people would realise.

The peaceful village of Caddington, located close to the M1 motorway two miles west of Luton town centre, does not immediately spring to mind as being a place for stories of the supernatural or for having connections with occult activity. Even less so a local beauty spot called Badgerdell Wood nestled just to the north

along a bridal track and known locally as the Bluebell Wood. However, this popular summer haunt, a short distance from the hustle and bustle of suburban Luton and within sight of the busy motorway, has been witness to two of the most unusual and frightening incidents to occur in Bedfordshire in recent times.

On 9 April 1963, police were called to Badgerdell Wood following a gruesome discovery made by two twelve-year-old Luton schoolboys. The police subsequently sent for local RSPCA Inspector, John Goodenough, who on arrival was horrified at the scene presented to him. Underneath bushes were the heads of six cows and a horse, all of which had been horrifically mutilated: the jaws had been wrenched apart, with two of the jawbones removed; the eyes had been completely severed and all had been cut out neatly as if by a surgeon's knife; while the heads themselves had been terribly battered and holes riddled the craniums, leading the Inspector to believe they had been shot to death. John Goodenough, a giant of a man at 6ft 8in and not one to be easily shocked, spoke of feeling 'revolted … absolutely physically sick' at the discovery. The incident had all the hallmarks of the now well-documented animal mutilation phenomenon, but this was 1963 and Snippy the horse, discovered in Alamosa, Colorado and reputed to be the first case of its kind, did not occur until much later in 1967. There was also a further puzzling factor for both the police and RSPCA – there was no sign of the bodies.

An important factor distinguishes the Caddington incident from a classic animal mutilation case in that there was definite human involvement. As Goodenough surveyed the scene with police officers, he discovered one of the eyeballs suspended from a branch overlooking two 9ft circles made from trampled-down grass. Within one of the circles was a gnarled tree that the Inspector believed may have served as a makeshift altar, and there was also evidence of a fire. Coming just three weeks after the discovery of the alleged Black Mass at nearby Clophill, rumours of witchcraft in the county were rife, leading Goodenough to conclude '…there is absolutely no sensible or logical reason for the heads being hidden in the wood. The only thing that I can think of is that it is tied up with the Clophill Black Magic in some way.' Enquiries carried out at farms within a fifty-mile radius to find out if any had reported missing cattle drew a blank. The incident, although reported briefly in the press of the time, including the *Daily Express* of 11 April, went practically unnoticed by many and, even today, elder residents of Caddington

do not recall the case. Was the 'Caddington Horror' a forerunner to the whole animal mutilation phenomenon of recent times? Sixteen years later, the Bluebell Wood seemingly gave up more of its sinister secrets.

Colby Pope was just nine years old in 1979 when, during the school summer holidays, he and several other children witnessed something at Bluebell Wood that, in Pope's own words, '[I] absolutely cannot explain' and prefers not to speak about, 'because you end up sounding like a complete nut.' Along with his two teenage sisters and three other friends, Pope embarked on a summer picnic into the countryside on the immediate outskirts of Luton. From Runley Road the group clambered through a hole in the iron grating that led into the M1 underpass and continued on beyond into the corn

Badgerdell Wood, also known as the Bluebell Wood, overlooking the M1 motorway on the outskirts of Caddington. As well as the alleged sighting of a strange cryptid creature, the area has been the scene of sinister occult activity since the early 1960s. (Kevin Gates)

fields surrounding the looming trees of Bluebell Wood. Settling down in a grassy spot away from the criss-crossing paths, they were halfway through their picnic when one of the group, Gary, stood up, having seen something standing in the trees nearby. As he stared and pointed, his face turned white. Years later, when interviewed by Kevin Gates, Pope would recall: 'We didn't know what was wrong with him, but we all turned and looked.'

A figure had emerged from the undergrowth and was just a short distance away. What the children saw at that moment and in broad daylight was to haunt each of them for many years afterwards. 'It was about 8ft tall, a dark brown-black creature. It had weird red glowing eyes, pointed ears on top of its head and huge wings,' Pope, now in his forties, remembered. He continued to describe the creature, noting, 'There was a yellow glow at its feet and it appeared to hover, or fly steadily. I can only describe it as a cross between a man, a bird and a bear.' The bizarre creature seemed to be interested in the picnickers and the group, unable to comprehend what they were seeing, were now understandably becoming distressed and frightened. The apparition began moving towards them using a strange gliding motion, almost as though it were levitating on the yellow light at its base. As one the group bolted but according to Colby Pope, like something from a nightmare, the creature seemed to have instilled some kind of control over them. 'It seemed impossible to run, almost like we were being pulled back towards it,' he told Kevin Gates. Despite this, the group managed to break through the treeline of Bluebell Wood and out into the adjacent corn field. As Pope looked back, he could see the yellow glow staying within the trees and skirting around the

The bizarre 'owlman' of Badgerdell Wood, seen by a group of Luton children during a daytime picnic in 1979. (Julian Vince)

edge of the wood.

The group were panic-stricken, yet only yards away vehicles sped along the busy motorway, oblivious to the drama unfolding below the raised embankment. Finally Pope and his friends made it to the other side of the field and rushed back through the underpass towards Runley Road. Clambering back through the iron grating they found to their immense relief that the opening in the metalwork was just big enough for all of them to get through, but too large for the creature still in pursuit. Finally they all made it through and ran out of the motorway underpass to what proved to be the safety of Luton's ordinary suburban streets. '[W]e heard the huge iron grate being shook [*sic*] behind us and an awful screeching noise amplified by the tunnel' recalled Pope, but the six youths had escaped.

Even today, Colby Pope is troubled by the incident. 'I'll never forget how terrifying the whole thing was and my sister and I occasionally talk about it.' His fantastical account would no doubt be derided by many as the invention of imaginative young minds, or perhaps could even be put down to mass hysteria. Yet Pope, his sisters and their companions that day are much older now and adamantly maintain that what they saw was real.

What actually happened in the peaceful Luton countryside on that summer afternoon in the late 1970s? The sighting of the creature at Bluebell Wood would appear to be similar to the American 'Mothman', or its British equivalent, 'Owlman', a frightening feathered humanoid creature seen in the vicinity of Mawnan Church in Cornwall in 1976 and again in 1978, one year before the experience of Colby Pope and his friends. The description given by Mr Pope certainly suggests the very same creature and when Pope was shown a sketch of the Cornish Owlman from 1976 by Kevin Gates, he remarked, 'It's very similar to what I saw.' The most famous recorded sighting of the Mothman was at Point Pleasant, West Virginia from November 1966 to December 1967, when the creature was witnessed by over one hundred adults as well as many children, some even standing face-to-face with the creature. During this period, there were also a number of bizarre animal mutilations in the area. In his book *The Mothman Prophecies* (1975), John A. Keel reports on a number of mysteriously killed cows, horses and dogs in the Point Pleasant area at the time of the sightings. These animals had 'surgical-like incisions in their throats' and 'often the carcasses seemed drained of all blood.' As such, the link to the 1963 incident at the same wood is an interesting one.

After speaking with Mr Pope, Kevin Gates felt confident that he had no prior knowledge of either the Mothman or Owlman phenomenon, and at such a young age certainly knew nothing of John Goodenough's dreadful discovery in 1963. Evidence from the Point Pleasant incident, as well as other sightings of Mothman, confirm that animal mutilations are frequently reported in the vicinity of these disturbing outbreaks. Had Mothman been visiting the Bluebell Wood for some years? Was a Satanic cult responsible for bringing the severed heads there as an offering forming part of an unknown ritual or ceremony? The wood was certainly well known locally as a meeting place for alleged devil-worshippers during the 1980s. Until further information comes to light, Bluebell Wood keeps its sinister secrets to itself and perhaps visitors today should treat this place with respect and caution.

Leagrave, like a number of villages on the outskirts of pre-twentieth century Luton, including Limbury, Biscot and Stopsley, was suburbanised by the expansion of the town from the end of the Victorian era through into the early decades of the 1900s. Leagrave Marsh, an open area of low-lying land adjacent to Leagrave Common and created by the joining of the fledgling river Lea with the tributaries which make up Knapps Brook, has been a place of habitation since Mesolithic times. Five thousand years ago the first permanent settlement was established here, surrounded by the Waulud's Bank earthwork which survives in part to this day amidst the sprawl of the Marsh Farm estate. The riverside was at one time a popular recreational area for local people and, despite the creation of a number of surrounding inter-war and post-war housing estates, the area remains open and is enjoyed by the public along the winding course of the river Lea at this point, much of the area being given over to allotments and open space. The site of the former Three Horseshoes at Leagrave, now a McDonald's restaurant, was at one time regarded as having a ghostly reputation, and Leagrave Marsh is also known as a haunted place.

Early one morning in 1968, seventeen-year-old Janice Whitmarsh together with a friend were making their way to work in nearby Sundon Park after staying overnight at a house in Marsh Road. It was cold and frosty and there were few people around as the two women passed by The Three Horseshoes pub. They decided on a short cut towards Sundon through the quiet and still expanse of Leagrave Marsh, where they found a layer of mist hung low over the grass and reed beds close to the riverside. As they approached the large playing field bordering the course of the river Lea,

Janice and her friend noticed two boys playing on the grass about 25–30ft away from where they were walking. Despite the early hour, the only thing that struck them as being slightly unusual was the somewhat old-fashioned way they were dressed, in short trousers and both wearing flat cloth caps. As the women continued walking the children, who seemed unconcerned by the coldness of the morning, were in plain view for about a minute before both Janice and her companion realised the two boys were becoming indistinct and in fact had quickly faded from sight. It was at this point, as the watchers realised that the figures were in fact apparitions, that they also became aware that both children were barefoot. 'I can see it as if it was yesterday,' Janice Whitmarsh, now Mrs Newitt, who

Lonely Leagrave Marshes, where the ghosts of two barefooted children were seen playing in the late 1960s. (Eddie Brazil)

today lives on Hayling Island, told me. 'We watched them playing for about a minute, then they [saw] us and faded out.' For the two women it was simply another early morning start for work and neither had any thoughts of ghosts or the supernatural on their minds at the time.

As discussed earlier in this book, the collective nature of Janice Whitmarsh's experience gives this account more credibility but, as with all reports of apparitions and similar paranormal experiences, how can we explain the Leagrave Marsh ghost children? Were they the spirits of two long dead Luton schoolboys, or something else? Paranormal theories that do not involve ghosts being the spirits of deceased people mostly interpret this kind of experience either in terms of some form of astral or telepathic projection, or psychic recordings imprinted in the environment of a particular place or location. This latter explanation, the so-called 'stone tape' theory, was championed by psychical researcher Tom Lethbridge (1901-71), a Cambridge don who has been described as the 'Einstein of the paranormal'. Lethbridge, a radical thinker whose writings on the paranormal involve an eclectic combination of archaeology, dowsing, scientific method and witchcraft, argued that all ghosts are images produced by the mind of the percipient rather than discarnate spirits or 'entities', and once stored in the psychic fabric of a building or location can be played back like a video recording due to some specific factor or combination of factors – the presence of a 'psychic' person, atmospheric conditions, etc. Many reported ghost sightings, where the figures or apparitions seem unaware of or are oblivious to the percipient or percipients and appear to be carrying out a set task or activities that originally took place years in the past, such as the vision of the two bare-footed boys playing by the river Lea, could be explained by this theory.

The creation of apparitions by telepathic projection also rules out the presence of spirits of the departed. There is evidence that some ghosts can be caused by the strong mental desire by a particular living person to be present in a different location or place other than where they are currently situated. An example of this kind of projected apparition is given by Ghost Club member Bowen Pearse in his book *Ghost Hunter's Casebook* (2007) and involves the late paranormal researcher Andrew Green. In the early 1970s, Green, a fanatical gardener, sold a house with a one-acre plot of land and moved to the village of Iden in East Sussex. Several months later, when the new owner, an engineer and his family, visited Green in his new home, his daughter (who had not met the ghost hunter before) claimed that she had seen his apparition, solid and lifelike, standing and walking in his former garden on a number of occasions. Green admitted that he missed his old house, particularly the garden and a large rockery that he had built himself and about which he often reflected about being able to tend again. If this line of thinking is correct, the two ghost boys seen by Janice Whitmarsh and her companion could have been the unconscious reminiscences of a living Lutonian whose vivid private thoughts about carefree former playtimes on Leagrave Marsh were somehow projected into the physical modern-day environment.

Some hauntings, however, have their origins firmly rooted in national legends and superstition. Forming a low silhouette on the horizon to the north-east of the town, visible to travellers passing along the nearby A6 trunk road and distinct from the neighbouring and much larger Warden Hill,

Galley Hill, where a gibbet stood during the sixteenth and seventeenth centuries. The area is said to be haunted by the spectral 'Hell Hound of Luton'. (Eddie Brazil)

lies Galley Hill, known to many Lutonians for its associations with the witchcraft purges of former times. Evidence of a possible witch cult was unearthed here in the early 1960s with the discovery of a buried horse's skull on top of which had been carefully placed a bone die with the number 'six' facing uppermost. A permanent gibbet was erected here in the sixteenth and seventeenth centuries when the land formed part of Stopsley Manor and as such the hillside saw a number of executions and the interment of local felons, as well as the victims of the superstitious beliefs prevalent throughout England at that time. The name Galley Hill is derived from 'Galowehil', meaning literally 'a hill with gallows'.

An example of the fevered atmosphere of those dangerous days, when any non-conformist villager, local wise woman or countryman against whom a neighbour held a grudge could find themselves being denounced for being in league with the Devil and casting spells, is given by the sorry tale of Elizabeth Pratt, a Dunstable widow

who along with three other local women, Mary Poole, Ursula Clarke and Mary Hudson stood trial at the Bedford Assizes in the spring of 1666 all accused of 'bewitching small children to death'. Despite a wealth of accusations and counter-accusations, including claims that Elizabeth was visited by the Devil in various forms including that of a man, a woman and a cat, no convictions were recorded. However, the following year, Elizabeth together with Mary Hudson and Ursula Clarke were again brought before the justices, charged with the murder of two boys who had died eighteen months before of 'a strange distemper'. On this occasion Mary and Ursula were again acquitted but Elizabeth Pratt was not so fortunate and, found guilty, she later died in gaol. Details of many of these so-called 'witches', as well as the supposed crimes that sent them to their deaths, have become lost in the mists of time but, unknown to the seventeenth-century witch finders, Galley Hill was in fact no stranger to violent death and bloodshed.

In 1961, archaeological excavations carried out in a burial mound on the summit revealed the chilling reality of murderous events stretching back to the Roman occupation of Britain and beyond. In a shallow chalk hollow the jumbled parts of two male skeletons, a Neolithic burial dating from nearly 5,000 years ago, were recovered. The bodies had been chopped into pieces but the origins of this grim event remain obscure – possibly these young men were the victims of some form of New Stone Age sacrifice, or they had died natural deaths and been dismembered after death. Far more gruesome and disturbing were the contents of what is known as the Galley Hill 'slaughter pit', which was opened at the same time as the Neolithic grave. In their book *The Story of Luton* (1964), James Dyer, Frank Stygall and John Dony, describe the scene that revealed itself as the hilltop mound finally gave up its grisly secrets:

Excavations … revealed the grim spectacle of an old man who lay with his arm round the waist of an aged woman. She had been a cripple, and had lost her right leg during her life time. A young woman lay near by, her head and arm severed from her body by an oblique sword cut across her shoulder. Two young men shared the same shallow grave, one thrown on top of the other. Most poignant of all was the body of a woman flung face downwards above that of a man and beneath them both the trunk and limbs of a twelve years old boy, whose head lay some distance away. Perhaps a mother had watched her son and husband brutally murdered, before she was treated in the same barbaric fashion.

It seems likely that these hapless people were victims of the great uprising that took place in AD 367, when a combined force

Silent witnesses to brutal times: skeletons from the Galley Hill 'slaughter pit' recovered in the early 1960s.

of Picts, Scots and Saxons swept southwards over Hadrian's Wall and plundered the country as far as London, destroying and killing as they went.

As well as the gallows associated with witchcraft at Warden Hill, a second gallows site is known in the same locale. In the eighteenth century, the area around both Warden and Galley Hills became a known hideout for highwaymen, who were able to use its elevated position to their advantage in watching for coach traffic on the road below running between Luton and Bedford. At a spot a quarter of a mile north of Galley Hill beside the road running east towards Lilley, a gallows and gibbet was erected in order to deter footpads and the like from plying their trade in this part of the county, and there is an interesting ghost story attached to this particular location. In his *Memories of Warden Hill* (1986), Francis Walkley describes the apparition of a coach and four being pursued by a similarly ghostly highwayman along the Old Bedford Road at the foot of Galley Hill, which was seen by a local farmer. Walkley obtained the information from a Streatley resident, Robert Allen, who had lived in the parish since the early 1920s and knew its stories well, such as the local legend that in times gone by, a highwayman, known to have killed a local waggoner, was run to earth and buried about a mile from the Lilley Road gallows. A wooden stake was planted to mark the spot which subsequently took root and grew into a tree, known by several names including the 'German tree', 'Jerry's tree' as well as the 'Jerrmiah's tree'.

Ghost stories abound in locations with far less a brutal and bloody history than the wooded slopes of distant Galley Hill. With such violence and drama to draw upon, one might expect the alleged haunting associated with this site to involve some-

thing along the lines of Zealia Bishop's 1929 Lovecraft-influenced novella *The Mound*, which features reports of phantom figures and strange lights being seen on the eerie silent hilltop at certain times of the day and night accompanied by the cries of a ghostly re-enactment of the 'slaughter pit' killings. In fact the ghost of Galley Hill falls back on the traditional haunted gibbet scenario familiar with many former execution sites across the country involving, like many of these places, the appearance of a large black phantom hound, most commonly known to both ghost hunters and folklorists alike as 'Black Shuck'. There are many derivatives of this ghost-dog haunting, some of which are associated with gibbets and gallows, and they go by a number of striking and colourful local names. The North of England is known as the hunting ground of 'Padfoot', an animal the size of a donkey whose feet are turned backwards; in Lancashire a similar beast is called by a number of names including 'Trash', 'Striker' and the 'Boggart' which, when seen, utters a terrible screeching sound before sinking down into the ground and disappearing; in Northumberland and parts of Yorkshire the 'Barguest' is described as being a large black dog with blazing eyes, while 'Shuck' or 'Shag' haunts the cemeteries and graveyards of East Anglia on dark stormy nights, terrifying wayward travellers unlucky enough to cross its path with its single flaming eye. The legend of the 'Black Dog' ghost is most strong in the West Country where it is known from a number of locations including Uplyme in Devon and the Blackmoor Gate crossroads on Exmoor. One phantom hound that breaks the tradition, however, is the Scottish 'Lamper' that haunts the wilds of the Hebrides

Islands and whose appearance is considered to be an omen of approaching death. This ghostly dog is said to be white rather than the traditional black and to have no visible tail.

Luton ghost hunter William King has published a lengthy account of the 'Black Shuck' phenomenon in his *Haunted Bedfordshire* (2005) in which he includes an account of the Galley Hill ghost, known as the 'Hell Hound of Luton'. According to King, the haunting has its origins in an event that took place in the early 1700s when one stormy night a thunderbolt struck the Galley Hill gibbet, setting fire to the tar-soaked corpses hanging in their iron cages which burnt so fiercely that it seemed to observers watching from the villages below that the whole hill was ablaze. Amongst the flames what appeared to be a large black dog or hound was seen leaping and dancing until, with the hanging bodies and presumably the gibbets themselves reduced to ashes, the spectral creature gave out a terrible howl and vanished. From that time onwards, Galley Hill was known as a hunting ground (or haunting ground) for the Black Dog phantom which, according to King, returns to the spot on odd occasions, with deadly consequences for anyone brave or foolhardy enough to face the ghostly animal rather than turn and run away. Can there be any truth to this colourful story? The Galley Hill gallows may well have been struck by lightning and at a distance the smoke and flames from the resultant fire may have resembled a leaping animal. However, it seems most likely that the 'Hell Hound' has its roots in a countrywide belief in ghostly dogs haunting the sites of old gallows and crossroads (where gibbeted criminals were commonly hung in chains and suicides buried). Across the county

border near Tring, just such a haunting is associated with the gallows site at Gubblecote Cross where Thomas Colley was hanged in August 1751 for the murder of Ruth and John Osborne, local villagers whom many believed practiced witchcraft. As a whole, neighbouring Hertfordshire is a county with its fair share of phantom dog hauntings – as well as Gubblecote Cross, 'Black Dog' ghosts are also reported from the churchyards of both St Nicholas's Church at Stevenage and St Lawrence's Church at Bovingdon.

Are there ghosts today on lonely Galley Hill? For paranormal investigators and researchers attempting to obtain evidence of supernormal activity at allegedly haunted sites such as hillsides, woods, and open spaces including parks and cemeteries, the practicalities of holding effective and worthwhile vigils at such locations – particularly at night – can be extremely challenging. Many uncontrollable factors, such as the weather, passing vehicles, the noises and activity of birds and animals, as well as other natural factors including distant lights and sounds carried on the wind, make the experiences reported at such events highly subjective and open to much interpretation. In August 2009, enthusiastic members of the Luton Paranormal Society visited Galley Hill for a night-time investigation during which a séance was held near one of the hilltop tumuli. The group reported a number of incidents including the sound of footsteps walking on stones, the appearance of a circular orange light floating above a pathway, and a dragging sound; as well as a choking sensation and the presence of a bitter and angry personality, possibly that of a formal felon executed here on the gallows in times gone by.

To the south of Luton, close to the busy environs of what is now London Luton

The ruins of Someries Castle close to London Luton Airport, said to be haunted by the fifteenth-century ghost of Sir John Wenlock. (Eddie Brazil).

Airport, is another local site with both historical and paranormal associations. Surrounded by open farmland, Someries Castle is the erroneous title given to all that remains of a brick-built former fortified manor house, constructed by Sir John Wenlock in the early years of the fifteenth century. Wenlock, who was killed aged seventy-one at the Battle of Tewkesbury on 4 May 1471 during the Wars of the Roses, was an English soldier and politician who at one time served as High Sheriff of Bedfordshire and Buckinghamshire. He may have pulled down an earlier building which is known to have been built on the same site in the thirteenth century by William de Someries, who gave his name to what is now itself a picturesque ruin. Someries is considered to be one of the earliest brick buildings in England, although by the time Sir John began work in 1430, brickwork construction in the country was already over a century old. The manor house was in fact never completed and much of what did stand was demolished in 1742, so all that can be seen today is the former gatehouse and chapel which formed the north-west wing of the building. Some salvaged bricks were used in the construction of neighbouring farm buildings and it is worth mentioning that the Polish-born English novelist Joseph Conrad (1857-1924), whose 1903 novella *Heart of Darkness* was the blueprint for Francis Ford Coppola's Vietnam War epic *Apocalypse Now* (1979), lived in the adjacent farmhouse while writing his novel *Under Western Eyes* (1911).

The exterior of the Wenlock chapel in St Mary's church, Luton. A stained-glass window depicts Sir John Wenlock, the builder of Someries Castle. (Eddie Brazil)

The title of the former 1st Baron Wenlock survives in the naming of Wenlock Street in Luton's High Town, and there is a Wenlock Chapel in the twelfth-century church of St Mary's in the town centre, where a fine stained-glass window depicts Sir John bowing in an act of servitude to the Crown complete with flowing robes and broadsword. According to local tradition, this is apparently not all that survives of the builder of Someries Castle, as the ghost of Sir John Wenlock is said to haunt the ruins and former grounds of his old home, now much changed by the passage of many centuries. Tony Broughall reports that the apparition of a man in dark-coloured armour brandishing a sword is associated with the site, but that the ghost has also been reported as appearing in the form of a 'hazy grey figure'. When and where these sightings took place has not been recorded with any degree of certainty, leaving objective researchers to conclude that possibly the haunting of Someries Castle is a case of an English castle in need of a resident ghost. One violent incident that appears not to have left a psychic mark on the location is the murder of Jane Castle by her twenty-four-year-old husband Joseph, which took place close to the ruins on 8 August 1859 following an argument. Castle cut his wife's throat as she walked home to her parents' house and was hanged at Bedford Prison in March of the following year.

From the outskirts we move now to the centre of Luton to look at the ghostly history of one of the town's most well-known public places, Wardown Park. Close to the A6 New Bedford Road a mile-and-a-half north of the town centre, the park began life as the grounds of a private estate known as Bramingham Shott whose origins date back to the early 1800s. Much of the familiar landscaped parkland was laid out in 1875 by the then owner Frank Scargill, a Luton solicitor, who at the same time rebuilt the original farmhouse as the museum building which survives to the present day. The property has changed hands a number of times. The businessman and Liberal politician Halley Stewart (1838-1937) owned the park for a number of years and the name Wardown was adopted during this period. Stewart began his career in banking but in the 1870s founded an oil seed refinery based in London and Rochester. Later this was sold and Stewart became a successful brick magnate, initially through the firm of B.J. Forder & Son, who established a brickworks at Wootton Pillinge, a village two-and-a-half miles north of Ampthill in Bedfordshire; this was subsequently renamed Stewartby in 1937 in honour of the Stewart family's investment in the area. During the 1890s, Forders (who eventually became the familiar London Brick Co. in 1923) were also tenants of Wardown Park and in 1904 the house and its eleven-acre grounds were bought by two Luton councillors for £16,250, who subsequently sold the property in its entirety to Luton Council the same year for the same price. There followed a period of improvement to the parkland: paths were laid out, a bowling green added, trees planted and Wardown's principle feature, the ornamental boating lake, was created by widening the natural course of the river Lea at this point. However, Frank Scargill's former handsome private house, with its feature gables and decorative brick chimneys, was allowed to fall into disrepair due to a lack of Council funds. During the First World War, the building was adapted into a military hospital with the cellars being taken over for use as a makeshift mortuary. During the inter-war years, the various rooms were used as Council offices and a restaurant until, in 1931, the house was refurbished

Wardown Park Museum. Built in the mid-1870s, the 'housekeeper' apparition seen here by several people over the years dates from the time the building was used as a military hospital during the First World War. (Eddie Brazil)

and opened as a permanent museum chronicling the town's local history, including the prominent hat and car-making industries, as well as being home to several important county natural history collections. To this purpose it is still in use today, benefiting from a £1m National Lottery grant in June 2005 which allowed extensive restoration to take place, including reconstruction work to the original boathouse and drinking fountain as well as the rebuilding of the original Edwardian 'daisy chain' wall. With such a varied history stretching back over 200 years, it is perhaps unsurprising that Wardown Park Museum and its grounds are one of the most persistently haunted places in the whole of Luton, with a number of good authenticated instances of phenomena being reported there.

Reports of strange and unusual happenings, including footsteps and the sighting of phantom figures, have been received with some regularity from Wardown Park Museum and the park grounds over a period stretching back nearly 100 years. The first incidents are very much anecdotal in nature and date from the period that the British Army were resident at Wardown. On occasions both nurses and soldiers were said to have been startled by the sudden appearance of a female apparition carrying a bunch of keys which became known as 'the housekeeper'. None of these encounters appear to have been documented and it is unclear as to actually how many incidents actually took place and over what period of time, with the result that this period of ghostly activity at Wardown Museum has now passed without clear record from living memory. However, in 1955, two local heating engineers, Hugh Upton and Anthony Roberts, were working on servicing the boiler installation in the cellar area of the museum building. The cellar had no permanent lighting and the two men were working by the light from a temporary lead lamp which had been rigged up using an extension cable running down the stairway from the floor above and was only sufficient to illuminate the immediate area around the boiler itself. The museum at the time was closed to the public and the only other person in the building apart from Upton and Roberts was the then curator, Charles Freeman, who was working in his office upstairs. As the two men worked they suddenly became aware of the sound of very light footsteps in the confines of the cellar room accompanied by what they interpreted as the swishing of a lady's skirt. Looking up they both saw the figure of a tall woman wearing a dark-coloured dress emerge from the shadows around 10ft from where they were standing and almost immediately pass round a corner of the cellar walling and vanish out of sight. Startled the two engineers followed but the woman was nowhere to be seen and on investigation the curator had not been disturbed and was unable to offer an explanation for their experience.

The kind of experience reported by the two Luton men was not without precedent. Two years before, in 1953, Harry Martindale, an eighteen-year-old apprentice plumber was carrying out a similar job on the central heating installation in the cellar of the historic Treasurer's House close to York Minster when he experienced what is one of the most impressive ghost sightings of the twentieth century. A column of around twenty Roman soldiers including one on horseback, which materialised out of a brick wall close to where the youth was standing, walked in a procession across the width of the cellar area before vanishing into the wall opposite. The vision lasted nearly half a minute and the ghostly figures were only visible from knee-level upwards. Twenty years later, in the early 1970s, archaeological excavations in the same cellar area uncovered the Via Decumana, the original Roman road that the spectral soldiers had been walking along in Martindale's incredible paranormal vision.

A large amount of the reported phenomena at the Wardown Park Museum is associated with the underground cellar area of the building. In 1971, the 'housekeeper' apparition was again seen by two workmen attending to the museum's boiler during what would appear to be an emergency call-out. The unnamed men were in the museum at night outside of normal working hours when, like Hugh Upton and Anthony Roberts sixteen years before, they heard the sound of approaching footsteps which on this occasion seemed to be coming down the stairway from the floor above. One workman later claimed to have seen the figure of a tall woman wearing a long dark dress, with a key chain hanging from her belt, who briefly came into view, then turned and went back up the stairs without acknowledging either of the two workers. On investigation the only other person present in the building, a caretaker, was adamant that no one else had been allowed access into the museum while the men were working down in the cellar. Other visitors to the museum have reported unusual experiences and it is clear that the sinister cellars are not the only haunted areas of the building. On the first floor, visitors have sensed a hostile presence as though 'someone [was] urging you to get out and leave'. I have also spoken to one Luton resident who during a visit felt a sensation of being pushed and saw moving shadows in one of the first-floor rooms containing displays of children's toys.

An explosion of public interest in the practical investigation of the paranormal in the UK, which has gathered momentum since the end of the 1990s, has resulted in the establishment of many local ghost-hunting groups and societies across the country. Methods of investigation vary, but many combine a spiritualist approach with modern technology, employing both psychics and sophisticated electronic equipment during the course of vigils at allegedly haunted buildings and locations. The Anglia Paranormal Investigation Society (APIS) was founded – appropriately enough on Halloween night, 31 October 2002 – by Hertfordshire-based writer Damien O'Dell, the author of several regional paranormal books, who has a particular interest in Bedfordshire ghosts (and Luton hauntings in particular), having both descendants from the county and active involvement in local psychical research for over forty years. APIS has carried out a number of organised investigations across both counties including the Sun Hotel, Hitchin, known for the apparition of a claw-handed monk; Chicksands Priory at Shefford, dubbed by O'Dell as 'Britain's Most Haunted House'; Watford Library, where staff have reported unusual happenings; and the George Hotel at Silsoe, known for the apparition of a lady in grey thought appropriately enough to be that of Lady Elisabeth Grey of nearby Wrest Park. In May 2010, O'Dell and his APIS team held an all-night investigation at Wardown Park Museum, during which they all had a number of interesting and unusual experiences.

The eight-person APIS team arrived at the museum on a Friday evening at 9.30 p.m., after closing hours, in order to familiarise themselves with the layout of the building and set up various pieces of equipment. The team were also keen to get some initial impressions of the location. In order to try not to prejudice as much as possible any experiences and information received during the vigil, only Damien O'Dell, who acted as Team Leader for the investigation, had details of the museum's haunted history, including 'hotspots' of activity and sightings of the 'housekeeper' ghost. Paranormalists will be familiar with much of the team's physical equipment, which included digital still cameras, video cameras, sound recorders, temperature/humidity gauges and an EMF (electromagnetic field) meter, also known as a magnetometer, a device popular with researchers in order to measure localised alterations in both AC and DC electromagnetic fields; changes that have been suggested as possibly being linked to the presence of paranormal activity in haunted areas. O'Dell divided the APIS team into four two-person groups which rotated between four locations on watches lasting forty-five minutes interspersed with fifteen-minute breaks. The areas covered were the main staircase, the back staircase (formerly used by staff during the time the building was owned by the Stewart family), a library room and the basement cellar. The investigation began at 10 p.m. and concluded at 1.30 a.m. the following morning.

During the course of the APIS vigil, several of the team experienced apparent phenomena. While spending a watch period on the back staff staircase, Damien O'Dell, not normally receptive to psychic impressions, became aware of a melancholy feeling of sadness that had formed in the immediate area around him, the intensity of which gave him the spontaneous intuition that someone had committed suicide here in the past. This impression was later confirmed after the conclusion of the vigil by Roger Smith, one of the museum staff who was present during the course of the investigation: a female servant had hanged herself over the back stairs during the time that the building was a private house, something that O'Dell was totally unaware of, even though he was familiar with several aspects of the museum's haunted history. A knocking noise as well as the sound of a window slamming was heard by Sue Skipper, while Gary Beaver also obtained unusual sounds – four metallic taps – on a digital recorder while upstairs in the library.

Not surprisingly, several of the APIS researchers including Gary Beaver, Rob Rothwell, Joanna Botcherby and Damien O'Dell, reported unusual activity in the cellar area of the building. This comprised several light anomalies including a beam of light that flashed across the basement horizontally at waist level and appeared to pass through Rob Rothwell's body, and a tennis ball-sized light seen by Gary Beaver while sitting in the cellar in darkness, which swerved past him around shoulder height before vanishing. Damien O'Dell was aware of the sound of heavy breathing in different parts of the basement room and had a tactile experience of a breath of cold air on his face when the breathing noises were clearly audible. At one point, a heavy 'Darth Vader-like' exhalation of breath was clearly heard by two investigators in response to a spoken request for a sign or acknowledgement; this striking phenomenon was captured on Joanna Botcherby's tape recorder.

The landscaped gardens of Wardown Park are not without their own ghostly associations. The sound of footsteps, the most common of all audible phenomena, have been heard on occasion by visitors when they are alone in certain parts of the park,

particularly along the long tree-lined footpath that links the New and Old Bedford Roads in the vicinity of the children's playground. One visitor, whose identity is known to me, was walking along this path during the 1980s when she heard footsteps coming from behind and had a distinct impression of an approaching person. Looking round she was startled to see that no one was there and the footfalls themselves abruptly stopped. Feeling quite threatened, she ran out of the park onto the Old Bedford Road where the feeling quickly subsided. More recently, in 2006, two Luton men, Abdul Kalam and a friend Ash Ali, were walking through Wardown Park around 8 p.m. one winter evening when they both had an unnerving experience which they later related to Damien O'Dell. The night was cloudy but despite the lack of moonlight, both Kalam and Ali became aware, as they walked along beside the still expanse of the boating lake, of a dark figure on the opposite side of the water. Both men saw a 'tall, thin, black silhouette' which as it approached the lakeside resembled a person dressed in a dark cloak. As they both watched, the figure, which was moving at right-angles to them, continued to advance steadily forward through the metal railings enclosing the lake and seemingly started to come across the surface of the water towards them. At this point, Kalam and Ali became scared and ran in the opposite direction. What they actually saw that night has never been satisfactorily explained.

Two other areas of public open space in and around Luton have been the locations for more paranormal experiences for our survey. Pope's Meadow, a large rising area of common land with a wooded summit immediately to the east of Wardown Park and running alongside the Old Bedford Road, is a popular recreational spot and hosts the town's annual Bonfire Night

The long tree-lined path linking the New and Old Bedford Roads on the edge of Wardown Park, where inexplicable footsteps have been heard. (Eddie Brazil)

The ornamental lake at Wardown Park. In 2006 a sinister black-caped figure was seen here walking across the water by two Luton men. (Eddie Brazil)

fireworks display each year. It was here, in 1998, that long-time Luton resident Sarah Martin [pseudonym] had a similar experience to that of Janice Whitmarsh on Leagrave Marsh back in the 1960s. Sarah and her former husband Tony had taken their spaniel dog Lucy for a run on the Meadow and, having reached the wood at the top of the hill, had gone some way inside the tree line. Both Tony and the dog were in front of her when Sarah bent down to look at something on the ground. 'I looked up and there was this young boy in front of me,' she remembered. '[W]e just stood looking at each other. He looked very pale, then he just faded away and Lucy was in front of me with my husband.' The child looked around six or seven years old and had 'the look of the 1940s' about him. Unnerved by the incident, Sarah felt unable to remain in the trees and made her way out onto the open Meadow. If some ghosts or apparitions *are* the surviving personali-

ties of deceased persons, it may be that this young Luton schoolboy enjoys returning to a place that was a favourite playground in life, and remains so in the world beyond the grave. Sarah Martin, a down to earth, sensible person, was able to recall the incident to me with great clarity and was convinced that she not only saw this somewhat lonely-looking ghost, but that the apparition of the former Luton youngster was also, during that bizarre fusion of the two worlds, completely aware of her as well.

The *awareness* that ghostly figures show to their observers together with the level of interaction with those that experience paranormal phenomena, can be a way of classifying (in a basic way) the varying types of apparition, in the same way that UFOlogists use the 'close encounter' system first devised by American astronomer J. Allen Hynek (1910–86) for evaluating sightings of unidentified flying objects. As such, a Grade I apparition would be a classic 'stone tape' ghost that shows no awareness of its observer and appears like a playback of a psychic recording, such as the vision of the Leagrave Marsh ghost children; the ghost boy encountered by Sarah Martin at Pope's Meadow is a Grade II apparition, that reacts to the observer or shows awareness of being seen but does not speak; a Grade III apparition shows both awareness and also addresses the observer directly, such as the figure of the old man at the former Skefko works in Leagrave Road; a Grade IV apparition would combine the aspects of III with a definite interaction with our physical environment (although this interaction may not physically occur and could be an associated hallucination created by the observer), i.e. the way that the phantom hitch-hiker opened the door of Roy Fulton's Mini-van

and responded to his question on where he wanted to go; finally, a Grade V apparition would involve not only ghosts that show an awareness of being seen, but whose appearance also involves some shift or change in the environment itself, to such an extent that it is also experienced to some degree by the observer and becomes a part of the paranormal experience. This last class of apparitional encounter, a 'timeslip ghost', which brings aspects of its own environment with it, is comparatively rare, but they are reported nonetheless. During our interview for this book, Sarah Martin described to me just such an incident which is both thought-provoking and disturbing.

Timeslips, the creation of what amount to temporary displacements or 'windows' that seemingly give access to both past and future times, have become a reasonably

Pope's Meadow, Luton, where the ghost of a young boy in 1940s clothes has been encountered among the trees. (Eddie Brazil)

familiar concept in the public mind thanks to television programmes such as the long-running *Doctor Who*, the dinosaur-infested *Primeval* and (for those that can remember it) Irwin Allen's *The Time Tunnel*. The Fortean world, as well as the world of ghosts and hauntings, contains many examples of these alleged occurrences of which a number are regarded as controversial classics. The most famous of these, the Versailles case, has divided the opinions of researchers since details were first published 100 years ago. On a hot summer day in August 1901, two former principals of St Hugh's College, Oxford, Miss Moberly and Miss Jourdain, while visiting the gardens of the Petit Trianon, seemingly slipped back in time and walked through the grounds as they would have been during the reign of Louis XIV. The two women claimed to have seen buildings and garden features that were no longer in existence and encountered solid-looking apparitions of courtiers in authentic period clothing as well as the ghost of Marie Antoinette herself. Another notable case, this time a wholly audible timeslip, took place again in France, this time in 1951, when two English sisters-in-law heard what has been claimed to have been a ghostly re-enactment of the disastrous Allied raid on the German-occupied coastal town of Dieppe on 19 August 1942. The women reported the sounds of gunfire, dive-bombers, explosions and the cries of wounded soldiers, that corresponded with the actual times the real fighting took place nine years previously.

Other timeslips are less known but equally as baffling. In *The Mask of Time* (1978), Joan Forman, author of a number of paranormal-related books, describes the experience of a small seven year-old boy from Hanley, Staffordshire who, while playing truant from school in 1896, walked through a doorway in a wall at the end of a cul-de-sac and found himself in 'a different world, a small town with houses nothing like I had ever seen before'. Beyond the town the landscape sloped down into a valley and beyond it were low tree-covered hills. Eleven years later, the same boy, now a soldier assigned to the 4th Army Headquarters, entered a village called Misery in northern France and realised he was in the place of his earlier 'vision'. 'The landscape was exactly as I had found it before'. Even more bizarre was the discovery made, decades later when he visited his childhood home in the early 1960s: in his boyhood timeslip he saw the street through the archway named 'Windmill Street'; now the area had since been redeveloped and one new estate road was (and still is) called Windmill Street.

Stockwood Park, a public recreation space, riding centre and golf course on Luton's most southerly side, like Wardown Park to the north, began life as the grounds of a large country house, in this case the estate of the Crawley family, one of Bedfordshire's leading land-owning dynasties. Stockwood House was owned by the Crawleys until the outbreak of the Second World War, after which it saw use as a children's hospital before being bought by Luton Council in 1945. The elegant building was eventually demolished in 1964 and today only the former stable block and walled gardens remain. The site has been redeveloped with a new Discovery Centre museum and is the home of the Mossman Collection, the UK's largest assemblage of vintage horse-drawn vehicles.

In May 2011, Sarah Martin [pseudonym] together with her thirty-two-year-old daughter Lorraine and her granddaughter, aged three, visited the park early one afternoon and spent some time at the playground close to the cafeteria where the child played happily. Quite quickly, the two women noticed that the atmosphere appeared to be changing; in broad daylight the area had become completely silent and the people around them had faded away. 'They were there but they weren't there,' was the way Sarah described the scene to me. The three found themselves seemingly alone, at which point her granddaughter called out, saying she was scared of the 'nasty little girl' who was looking at her. The older woman could see nothing but her daughter Lorraine said she could see a child, aged between five or six, in old-looking clothes with an awful look of hostility on her face. How long the strange shift in the environment lasted was difficult for them to judge but Sarah Martin believed it was in total around five minutes. The eerie child was only visible for a short while and when both adults made a decision to move away in order to comfort their three-year-old, suddenly everything went back to normal; it was a warm afternoon and the playground area was again busy with families and their children.

How and why all of the strange happenings described in this chapter take place we are, at present, unable to explain. They are a compelling and unseen component of what is clearly, to paraphrase the mystical poet William Blake's famous description, 'England's green and pleasant – and haunted – land'.

six

UFO Connections

HE sighting of strange unidentified flying objects in the sky does not automatically equate to the presence of alien spacecraft or visitors from other worlds, in the same way that, as we have seen, the appearance of ghosts or apparitions is not proof of survival after death or the existence of a spirit world. In recent years, some UFOlogists and paranormal researchers have suggested that there may be a connection between reports of both UFO and ghost sightings in certain places; a link that previously would not have been considered by either factions of investigators in the Fortean world. Our survey of the strange and inexplicable in and around Luton concludes with a brief look at some of the surprisingly numerous accounts of unidentified flying objects and associated happenings that have taken place here over the last fifty or so years.

A number of areas around the UK are known as being particular UFO 'hotspots'. In Scotland they include Luce Bay and Stranraer in the south-west and the Lothian region around Edinburgh. It was here in November 1979 that a forestry worker near Livingston, a new town ten miles west of the city, had a frightening encounter with a daylight UFO which had come to ground in a clearing in the Dechmont Woods during a prolific 'flap' of UFO sightings in the area. In Wales, south-west Dyfed, particularly the coastline to the south and west of Milford Haven, is regarded by UFOlogists as being consistently rich for reported sightings as well as close encounters with apparent UFOnauts. A triangle of lonely Pennine moorland between Sheffield, Manchester and Leeds on the Lancashire-Yorkshire border is a highly regarded window area in England, while Warminster on the outskirts of Salisbury Plain gained notoriety in the 1960s for UFO activity and retains this reputation to this day.

Bedfordshire is not considered a notable centre for unidentified flying objects, but there can be no denying that unusual things have been reported here. American aviator Kenneth Arnold introduced the term 'flying saucer' into the public consciousness when, in June 1947, he observed nine shining disc-like objects flying in a chain formation in the sky near Mt Ranier, Washington. The United States Air Force officially listed Arnold's report as 'a mirage' but whatever the true explanation, the pilot's experience was instrumental in ushering in the modern UFO age which quickly took hold around the world. One of the first reported UFO sightings in Luton took place a year after Kenneth Arnold's encounter when an unnamed resident described seeing a burning comet-like object flying over the town at night. On Bonfire Night 1953, a long cigar-shaped 'craft' surrounded by a gaseous ring was reported by a farmer's son; the UFO eventually accelerated away at tremendous speed and was lost to sight.

In 1957, a group of school children together with their teacher saw a bizarre object in the sky over Ramridge Junior School in Stopsley on the northern outskirts of Luton. The incident made deep impressions on several of the young witnesses, so much so that fifty years later, despite the passage of nearly half a century, two of the boys were able to recall their experience vividly to a reporter from the *Luton News*. 'That day is something that's been in my memory all my life,' Steve Clarke remembered, describing a strange round object which seemed to hover in the blue sky over nearby houses and was clearly visible from the school field where Clarke's class were playing a game of rounders. 'I never saw it arrive or leave, but what I do remember quite clearly was a woman teacher on my right and four or five other kids to my left…and everybody just stopped. The teacher looked at us…alarmed.' The UFO, what would be termed a 'daylight disc' by researchers, has been variously explained as being either an airship or a floating weather balloon, but ultimately what really happened that day in the skies over Luton remains a mystery.

School children feature in another bizarre and unexplained incident that took place ten years after the Ramridge UFO sighting, this time in the Domesday village of Studham, on the Bedfordshire border six miles south-west of Luton town centre. On 28 January 1967, seven boys aged around ten years old, from the Studham Lower School, claimed to have encountered a blue-coloured dwarf-like humanoid figure in a grassy dell on Studham Common during an afternoon lunch break. When approached, the 'Blue Man' appeared and disappeared several times, each time vanishing into a cloud of yellowish-blue vapour that it seemingly appeared to be able to produce at will, accompanied by an eerie sound likened to that of 'non-human' voices. From the children's accounts published in local newspapers of the time, paranormal researcher William King has drawn up the following description: 'He had two round eyes, a triangle for a nose and was wearing a one-piece outfit with a broad black belt, at the front of which was a black box about fifteen centimetres square.

The 'Blue Man' of Studham, who appeared to a group of schoolchildren in 1967. The incident has never been fully explained. (Julian Vince)

It seems that his beard was split into two below his chin and ran down each side of his chest.' The figure was around a metre high and wore a tall rounded helmet. It reportedly kept its arms close to its sides but the bottom half appeared to be somewhat misty or apparitional, with the result that the boys were unable to describe the lower limbs or extremities in any detail. The children clearly experienced something that day, as those who interviewed the boys at the time were certain that they were not lying or hoaxing the school staff.

Was the 'Blue Man' of Studham an extra-terrestrial, a ghost from the future or something totally beyond our present understanding? Interestingly, in December 1987, twenty years after the incident on Studham Common, a former police officer claimed to have had a rare British close encounter of the third kind while crossing Ilkley Moor in the Pennine 'window area' mentioned previously. The anonymous witness saw a small greenish-blue figure around a metre tall which scuttled amongst rocks before fleeing to a white-coloured disc-shaped craft that then took off vertically and vanished into the sky. Before it made its successful escape, the retired officer managed to take a single photograph which shows the creature making its way up a barren hillside. Whether it is real or not is impossible to say, but the 'Ilkley Moor Alien' bears a passing resemblance to the eerie 'Blue Man' who seemingly appeared and disappeared in equally mysterious circumstances two decades before.

Five years before the strange 'Blue Man' incident, a Vauxhall delivery driver from Luton was involved in a frightening UFO encounter that took place on the B489 Lower Icknield Way at Tringford, two-and-

The controversial 'Ilkley Moor Alien', photographed by a former police officer in October 1987.

An impression of the UFO seen by Luton Vauxhall worker Ronald Wildman, during a night-time car journey through Tringford in February 1962. (Julian Vince)

a-half miles south-west of Ivinghoe. The incident is notable as it involves a close encounter of the second kind, i.e. a UFO sighting that contains some physical interaction with the immediate environment which is either felt or observed at the time of the incident, or is discovered and recorded at some point afterwards. This can involve disturbances to the ground, such as the impressions of a craft or spaceship landing or coming to earth, or interference affecting radios, car electrical systems or watches. In the early hours of the morning of 9 February 1962, Ronald Wildman left Luton to drive a new estate car from the Vauxhall car plant to a dealer in Swansea. The roads were deserted and it seemed the trip would be routine and uneventful. Around 3.30 pm, Wildman was driving along the Lower Icknield Road when, on the approach to a crossroads junction on the outskirts of Tringford, he saw a white oval-shaped object with black horizontal window-like markings or openings, hovering around 20-30ft above the level of the roadway ahead. Wildman estimated the object was in excess of 40ft wide and as he approached he suddenly felt the estate car begin to lose power – although the headlights remained on, the engine revs dropped off alarmingly so that despite pumping the accelerator and changing down through the gears, the car was soon crawling forward at less than twenty miles per hour. The sinister white object remained in front and above as the Vauxhall worker moved down the road for approximately 200 yards when, with no warning, a white haze similar to the familiar halo that often appears around a full moon, spread around its entire outline and it soundlessly took off at a tremendous speed, disappearing westwards in the direction of Aston Clinton; frost on the branches of the trees lining the roadway was knocked onto the windscreen of the car as it clipped the tree tops while passing overhead. Terrified, Ronald Wildman suddenly found the estate responding normally again and, as the engine began picking up, he drove in a state of complete panic to Aylesbury police station where officers took down a statement. His distraught character was apparent to the policemen who carried out the interview and they, as well as investigators from the London-based *Flying Saucer Review*, who subsequently met and interviewed the Luton man, were convinced he had had a genuinely frightening experience. What Ronald Wildman saw that day remains a mystery to this.

Warden Hill, like other prominent high-ground sites such as Chanctonbury Ring on the South Downs in West Sussex, is known for several mysterious and unexplained UFO sightings. In April 1974, what appears to be another close encounter of the second kind took place here when an unidentified object showing green, red and white lights was seen engaging in 'complex manoeuvres' in the night sky by a group of students directly over the hillside to the east of Luton. A second object was seen to land and later, according to a report in the *Luton Evening Post*, an area of scorched grass was found at what was suspected to be the landing site.

Ashcroft Park, within close walking distance of Ramridge Junior School, was the location for a strange incident which took place in 1975, and which is difficult to accurately assign to a specific category of paranormal experience. What at first could be described as a psychic UFO sighting also contains elements of angelic vision, as well as links with more traditional ghostly phenomena. Future Luton Paranormal Society founder and President Andrew Fazekas, then aged sixteen, together with a friend, was visiting the park on a cloudy afternoon; the time was around 1.00 p.m. when Fazekas became aware of an intense sensation of being watched or observed in some way. As the feeling steadily increased, he glanced up at a cloud mass directly over Ashcroft High School and was amazed to see two dark figures silhouetted against the clouds and from which this feeling of unearthly scrutiny appeared to originate. The vision lasted only a few seconds and as Andrew Fazekas turned towards his companion, he also had the fleeting impression of a 'disc'-like object in the same area of clouded sky as the bizarre figures; on turning back moments later the vision had disappeared and with it the eerie 'watched' feeling. The incident made a deep impression on the future ghost hunter, particularly as a fortnight later, while visiting Ashcroft Park again, this time at night, the two youths seemingly had an encounter with the headless apparition of a woman in white. Around 9 p.m., while standing together smoking cigarettes, the two youths noticed a white shape moving across the open recreation ground towards them. As it came closer both realised it was the tall figure of a woman in a flowing white Victorian dress; they could see the legs moving clearly beneath the material *but there was no impression or outline of a face or head*. When the figure got within 20ft of where they were standing, the nerve of both young men broke and they ran from the park.

Some UFOlogists and paranormal researchers have suggested a link may exist between the appearance of apparitions and UFOs at particular locations that are known both for hauntings and as 'window areas' of unidentified flying object activity. Pendle Hill near Burnley in the Pennine 'hotspot' is notorious amongst paranormalists of both disciplines for many spectacular UFO sightings (dating back in one instance to 1914), close encounters and even an alleged UFO abduction incident, as well as for witchcraft, curses and hauntings. The Pendle witch trials have become familiar to people with a mainstream interest in ghost hunting through a memorable 2005 Halloween episode of the controversial *Most Haunted* television reality series that featured supposed contacts with the spirits of lepers, witches and alien beings in equal measure. In his *Dark Journey* (2005), psychic investigator David Farrant, whose name is now synonymous with the Highgate Vampire case of the early 1970s, has suggested the possibility that ghostly phenomena occurring at haunted sites may be part and parcel of reported UFO sightings at the same locations, and that this haunting 'power' or 'energy' is actually being wrongly interpreted as flying saucers or unidentified flying objects. A small percentage of close encounters of the third kind claimants report contact with alleged alien beings taking place psychically through dreams or paranormal visions rather than actual physical meetings with UFOnauts, while alien contact also features in séances and physical mediumship experiments. I have attended a number of blackout physical séances over the past few years where the entranced medium has spoken as a personality claiming not only to be of extra-terrestrial origin but also as a 'collective' of the individual consciousness of numerous alien beings. As far-fetched as this may sound, there are precedents for this type of occurrence. In the mid-1960s, an experimental research organisation known as SORRAT (Society for Research on Rapport and Telekinesis) holding séance-type sittings under the direction of Prof. John Neihardt at Skyrim Farm in Missouri, experienced similar trance communication from a collective 'entity' that became known to them as 'Many Voices'.

There have been a number of UFO sighting reports that have been given prominence in the local media over the past few years. On 14 June 1997, a round black object the size of a small plane was seen early in the morning hovering over the town centre. After staying in a stationary position for a moment, it suddenly accelerated vertically away and disappeared. In 2008, a 'flap' of reported incidents in the Luton and surrounding area (as well as the UK as a whole) included accounts of mysterious sky lights over Leagrave, Houghton Regis and Eaton Bray. An unknown object was observed for nearly an hour in the vicinity of London Luton Airpot which, according to the official Ministry of Defence record of the incident, appeared to be monitoring air traffic from the airport. Lighting on a construction tower crane may have been misinterpreted in some cases, but a number of people who brought their sightings to the attention of the *Luton News* were adamant that what they saw could not be explained away so easily. The area and countryside around Warden Hill continues to attract strange and inexplicable objects. In January 2011, Jane Rutherford [pseudonym] saw a bizarre bird-like object hovering in the midday sky over her house at the Bushmead end of the Old Bedford Road and within clear sight of Warden Hill. The object was approximately 10ft across and had a circular silver centre with two wing-like projections on either side that each tapered to a narrow point. These 'wings' were black in colour with a silver underside. The appearance of the object was accompanied by a loud buzzing noise as it drifted towards the observer's garden and was visible for some minutes before disappearing as quickly and mysteriously as it had appeared. The strange noise also vanished with the object. A 'daylight disc' or a 'psychic UFO'?

In the last quarter of the twentieth century the crop circle phenomenon has become linked with the appearance of UFOs and the possibilities of alien contact. Swirled circle-shaped disturbances were first reported on a number of occasions in crop fields in Queensland, Australia, as well as farmers' fields in Warminster, England in the mid-1960s and immediately were considered to be evidence of alien landing sites. Paranormal researcher Andrew Collins has claimed that the phenomenon is in fact much older and that 'fairy rings' that we would nowadays describe as crop circles were reported in neighbouring Hertfordshire as early as the latter part of the seventeenth century. The late Betty Puttick, a folklorist and writer on paranormal subjects, was the first person to bring to the attention of UFOlogists the existence of a rare pamphlet dated 1678 entitled *The Mowing Devil: Or, Strange News out of Hartfordshire*. The pamphlet described the activities of an 'infernal

The 'Mowing Devil' from a seventeenth-century Hertfordshire pamphlet. Some UFOlogists have cited the incident as an early example of the crop circle phenomenon.

The strange daylight UFO, which was seen hovering over a house in the Old Bedford Road close to Warden Hill. (Julian Vince)

spirit' which created a strange glow in the night sky. The next morning, a flattened area of oat crop was discovered, 'so neatly mow'd by the Devil … that no Mortal Man was able to do the like'. Collins has also collected other twentieth-century accounts which pre-date the modern era of crop circle reports, including a circle seen in Kent in 1918, another from Aberystwyth in West Wales in 1936 and other circles from Hampshire encountered by a farmer in the 1940s.

Although crop circles and similar formations are a worldwide occurrence, the vast majority of reported incidents (estimated as being as much as 90 per cent) have taken place in the south of England with Wiltshire and Hampshire being particularly affected with strange and seemingly mysterious formations. However, the paranormal nature of these crop circles was severely damaged in the early 1990s when two Englishmen, Doug Bower and Dave Chorley, admitted to having hoaxed researchers and the media by creating over 200 circles around the country throughout the 1980s. Today most scientists, as well as many UFOlogists, attribute the continuing appearance of twenty-first-century crop circles to a combination of fraud and weather effects.

Luton's most notable crop circles have occurred in the vicinity of Dunstable Downs and the village of Barton-le-Clay, six miles to the north of the town centre, and have been most visible from the heights of the impressive Sharpenhoe Clappers escarpment, itself considered by some to have ghostly associations. A bizarre crescent-shaped formation appeared at Barton on 6 August 1996. In July 2000, local interest in a series of concentric circles which appeared at the base of Dunstable Downs was increased by reports of amateur video footage taken at the site that contained footage of a ball of bright white light moving rapidly around the field in the vicinity of the disturbed crops. Three years later, in July 2003, a large crop circle, formed around a pentagram-shaped design, was discovered in a field close to Sharpenhoe village. Barton-le-Clay was the scene of another incident in the autumn of 2008 when a second five-sided crop 'circle' surrounded by two crescent rings appeared in a cereal field at Barton Hill Farm. The area around Barton, with the Sharpenhoe hills in close proximity, has a reputation for a number of UFO incidents over the years. In July 2006, the Ministry of Defence catalogued four bright independent orange lights that were seen travelling north from Luton towards Bedford. What these – and many of the other incidents looked at in this chapter – really were, is something that will in all probability remain an enigma.

seven

A Luton Ghost Walk

OUR survey of Luton's haunted heritage comes to a close with a suggestion for a ghost walk around parts of the town centre, picking up a number of sites with paranormal connections along the way. The walk starts and finishes in St George's Square and, covering three-and-a-quarter miles, at a leisurely pace would be ideal for a Sunday morning. It can be shortened if there isn't time for a ghost hunting marathon all in one go, and the Wardown Park loop is quite suited for a separate outing all of its own. The figures in square brackets correspond with a location marked on the map. Nearly all of the haunted stops along the way are included in this book and it's worth taking a camera with you as spontaneous encounters with the paranormal can happen, as we have seen, when you least expect them ...

Starting in St George's Square with the Central Library behind you, to your right is [1] the Galaxy, the multi-screen cinema and leisure complex. Opened in 1998 on a plot of land originally used as the Crown and Anchor brewery, it is of interest to paranormalists through reports of a shadowy figure, seen moving by staff members around Screen 6 of the Cineworld section of the building. Workers in this part of the cinema have also heard unusual noises and there have been accounts of sensations of sudden coldness being experienced as well.

Walk around the corner of the Galaxy building into the start of the New Bedford Road and directly opposite the cinema on the corner of Alma Street is Cresta House, an office block built on the site of the former [2] Alma Theatre. Parts of the old building, demolished in the 1960s, had a reputation for being haunted by an unseen presence that seemed to follow members of staff around. There were also reports of people being pushed down the staircase at the rear of the theatre. The Alma was deemed an unlucky building and stories of a curse affecting the site were common in Luton in years gone by. Continue past Cresta House and turn into Inkerman Street. Look out for [3] No. 43 as you walk up the road. The original house has been demolished and rebuilt but Tony Broughall, Luton's first dedicated ghost hunter, lived here as a young man; Jesse John Hunt, a prominent Luton Spiritualist, was a lodger at this address for a number of years.

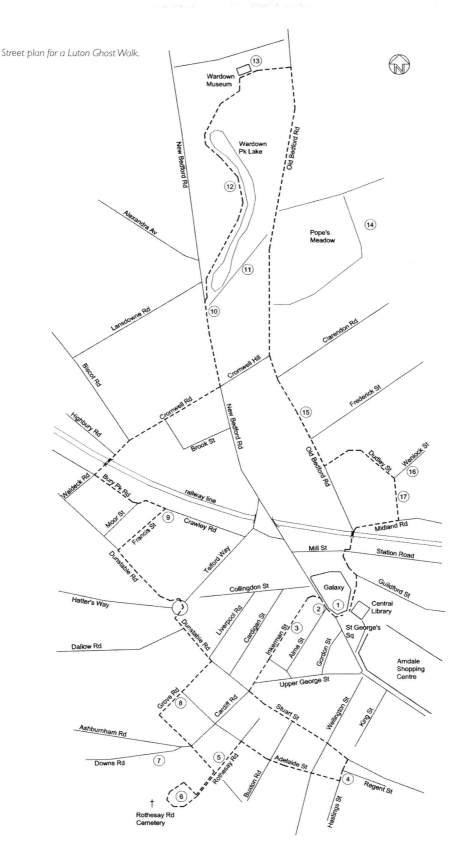

Street plan for a Luton Ghost Walk.

Continue up Inkerman Street, go over the traffic light crossing and turn left into Stuart Street. Walk past the Police Station and the Magistrates' Court until you reach Hastings Street. On the corner with Regent Street is the [4] BBC Three Counties Radio building. Investigations have been carried out here by both the Luton Paranormal Society and the Anglia Paranormal Investigation Society following reports of the apparition of a woman seen standing in the reception area. Walk up Hastings Street and take the first right into Adelaide Street; continue along here until you reach the crossroads junction with [5] Rothesay Road and turn left. In an unidentified house on this street (which may possibly be one of the older buildings still standing), physical medium Jack Webber gave a blackout séance shortly before the outbreak of the Second World War during which he was allegedly levitated and turned upside down, leaving a shoe mark on the ceiling.

No ghost walk should be without a visit to a burial ground or graveyard, so continue up the hill and go through the entrance gates of the [6] Rothesay Road Cemetery. The cemetery commands a good view out over the town so this would be a good vantage point for watching UFO activity during a night walk. Leave the cemetery by the same gate, go a short way back down Rothesay Road and turn left into Napier Road. Stop for a moment at the crossroads junction ahead. A little way up Ashburnham Road, on the left, is the turning into [7] Downs Road. This area was known in the 1920s for sightings of a female apparition that became known as the 'White Woman of Downs Road'. Leave Napier Road, cross straight over and go down Grove Road. Look out for the [8] Luton Spiritualist Church as you go round the block, then follow the

road down until you can turn left onto the main A505 Dunstable Road. Walk past the St Mary's Nursing Home on your left, and then take the pedestrian walkway over the roundabout so that you come down on the Bury Park side and continue under the new tramway bridge up Dunstable Road.

Turn right into Francis Street. The area now occupied by the Sainsbury's and Lidl supermarkets was originally the site of the old Luton gas works. Walk up Francis Street until you reach the [9] junction with Crawley Road. It was here that an employee saw a bizarre Amazonian ghost woman drifting up Crawley Road in 1961. Turn left into Crawley Road and follow it round into Bury Park Road; then go right into Waldeck Road and under the railway bridge. This is the route that the apparition took before vanishing in the vicinity of Highbury Road, which is the first on the left.

Carry on down Waldeck Road until you come to the traffic light junction with the A6 New Bedford Road. You can shorten the walk at this point by turning right and following the New Bedford Road back into the town centre and into St George's Square again. If you're up for a marathon ghost tour then turn left and go down the New Bedford Road until you reach the first entrance way into [10] Wardown Park on the right. The [11] long straight tree-lined avenue that goes from the park entrance at this point along the right-hand side of the lake and connects with the Old Bedford Road is the path where eerie footsteps have been reported by park visitors. Keep to the left hand side of the water and follow the path around the edge of the boating lake. Near the [12] bridge that crosses the lake, a strange black figure was seen during a night time visit by two Luton men in 2006. Carry on round the lake and make your way to [13] Wardown Park Museum, one of Luton's most haunted buildings. There have been several sightings of a female apparition in the basement area but this is off-limits to visitors. However, a number of people have experienced strange impressions of invisible presences in the public areas, particularly on the first floor, so it is worth spending some time here taking in the atmosphere.

Once you've checked out the museum, make your way out of the park onto the Old Bedford Road and follow it back towards the town centre. As you pass [14] Pope's Meadow on your right, spare a thought for the ghost boy in 1940s school clothes who has been seen in the trees at the top of the field. Carry on down the Old Bedford Road. At the rear of No. 90, Old Bedford Road was the former [15] Clegg & Holden printing works where a number of strange incidents of a paranormal nature were regularly reported going back to the early 1950s. The disturbances were thought to centre around a former owner of the business, with the result that the ghost became known as 'Old Cleggie'. Over the years, staff reported lights being switched on and off at night, objects moving on their own, including the shattering of a glass mirror, and the appearance of the apparition of 'a slim man about fifty with a sunken face and wearing a grey suit', thought to be 'Old Cleggie' himself, who was last seen in 1975. When you reach the English Rose pub, turn left into North Street and follow it round the corner into Dudley Street, then go down to the roundabout junction with [16] Wenlock Street on the left. This is named after Sir John Wenlock whose ghost is said to return to his former home, the lonely ruins of Someries Castle on

The rear of the former printing works of Clegg & Holden in the Old Bedford Road, where a well-known haunting took place during the mid-1970s. (Eddie Brazil)

the outskirts of the town close to London Luton Airport. As you continue along Dudley Street there is a narrow alleyway leading off to the left. This leads into [17] Albion Road where at one time a house (now demolished) was affected by poltergeist phenomena. Turn right out of Dudley Street into Midland Road and then turn left into the Old Bedford Road, go under the railway bridge and make your way round the front of the Galaxy centre back into St George's Square.

Wherever you walk in Luton, the many and varied cases in this book prove that there is a good chance that you may encounter some aspect of the paranormal. If you are lucky enough to encounter a ghost or have an unusual experience, I would welcome details to include either in a future edition of this book or in a sequel volume. Please feel free to contact me, either via the publisher, The History Press, or direct at The Limbury Press: www.limburypress.co.uk.

Select Bibliography and Further Reading

Adams, Paul, Brazil, Eddie & Underwood, Peter, *The Borley Rectory Companion* (The History Press, Stroud, 2009); *Shadows in the Nave: A Guide to the Haunted Churches of England* (The History Press, Stroud, 2011)

Austin, William, *The History of Luton and its Hamlets (Two Volumes)* (The County Press, Newport, 1928)

Brealey, Gina & Hunter, Kay, *The Two Worlds of Helen Duncan* (Regency Press, London, 1985)

Broughall, Tony & Adams, Paul, *Two Haunted Counties: A Ghost Hunter's Companion to Bedfordshire & Hertfordshire* (The Limbury Press, Luton, 2010)

Collins, Andrew, *The Circlemakers* (ABC Books, Leigh-on-Sea, 1992)

Crossley, Alan E., *The Story of Helen Duncan: Materialization Medium* (Arthur H. Stockwell Ltd., Ilfracombe, 1975)

Dyer, James, Stygall, Frank & Dony, John *The Story of Luton* (White Crescent Press, Luton, 1964)

Edwards, Harry, *The Mediumship of Jack Webber* (Rider & Co., London, 1946)

Farrant, David, *Dark Journey* (British Psychic & Occult Society, London, 2005)

Farson, Daniel, *The Hamlyn Book of Ghosts in Fact and Fiction* (Hamlyn, London, 1978)

Forman, Joan, *The Mask of Time: Mystery Factor in Timeslips, Precognition and Hindsight* (MacDonald & Jane's Publishing, Ltd., London, 1978)

Goss, Michael, *The Evidence for Phantom Hitch-Hikers* (The Aquarian Press, Wellingborough, 1984)

Grabham, Eddie, *From Grand to Grove: Entertaining South Bedfordshire* (The Book Castle, Dunstable, 2007)

Keel, John A., *The Mothman Prophecies* (Saturday Review Press, New York, 1975)

King, William H., *Haunted Bedfordshire: A Ghostly Compendium* (The Book Castle, Dunstable, 2005)

O'Dell, Damien, *Paranormal Bedfordshire* (Amberley Publishing, Stroud, 2008)

Pearse, Bowen, *Ghost Hunter's Casebook: The Investigations of Andrew Green Revisited* (Tempus Publishing, Stroud, 2007)

Randles, Jenny, *UFOs & How to See Them* (Anaya Publishers Ltd., London, 1992)

Tyrrell, G.N.M., *Apparitions* (Gerald Duckworth & Co. Ltd., London, 1953)

Underwood, Peter, *The Ghost Hunter's Guide* (Blandford Press, Poole, 1986)

LOCAL PARANORMAL GROUPS

Luton has its own dedicated ghost hunting organisation, the *Luton Paranormal Society*, founded by their President, Andrew Fazekas, in 2003. The LPS has a programme of investigations throughout the year and details of their work, as well as a comprehensive survey of ghostly phenomena throughout the counties of Bedfordshire, Hertfordshire and Buckinghamshire, can be found on their website: *www.lutonparanormal.com*.

A Hertfordshire-based ghost-hunting organisation with an interest in Luton and Bedfordshire hauntings is Damien O'Dell's *Anglia Paranormal Investigation Society (APIS)*. APIS is always keen to involve serious-minded people with an interest in the paranormal in their investigations. Details can be found on their website: *www.apisteamspirit.co.uk*.

NATIONAL PARANORMAL ORGANISATIONS

For anyone involved in serious research into the paranormal, membership of the following three British societies should be considered. They are the *Ghost Club: (www.ghostclub.org.uk)*, founded in 1862; *ASSAP*, the *Association for the Scientific Study of Anomalous Phenomena: (www.assap.ac.uk)*, founded in 1981: and the *SPR*, the *Society for Psychical Research: (www.spr.ac.uk)*, established in 1882. Their publications and archives contain invaluable information and resource material, much of which is now being made available online.

Index